T0331204

Intelligent Infrastructure

With the development of sensor technology, wireless communications, big data, and machine learning, there is an increasing interest in technologies and solutions that assess and predict the state of equipment and assets within various industrial settings. These technologies aim to collect information from multiple sources about infrastructure asset status. Then, through current and historical data analysis, this configuration of technologies delivers intelligence on current and future asset status to a maintenance operator or manager to inform optimal maintenance decision-making. These technologies are known under different terms – remote condition monitoring, e-maintenance, prognostic systems, predictive maintenance, and smart or Intelligent Infrastructure. Despite the promise of remote condition monitoring and predictive technologies, there is a growing concern with such technologies because they can be difficult or impractical to use.

Understanding and mitigating potential human factors issues could ensure that such vast investments are not wasted. This book considers, in depth, the challenges placed on users of current and future condition monitoring systems. Its primary focus is to understand the cognitive processes, including managing alarms, interpreting data, and collaborating with automation. The book describes a range of human factors methods that can be used to understand the current and future functioning of people and technology in an enhanced maintenance and asset monitoring context. The book also presents a framework for describing these issues systematically and presents the resulting design considerations to increase the effectiveness of individual operators and organisations as a whole.

Intelligent Infrastructure

User-Centred Remote
Condition Monitoring

Nastaran Dadashi

David Golightly

Sarah Sharples

Richard Bye

CRC Press
Taylor & Francis Group
Boca Raton London New York

CRC Press is an imprint of the
Taylor & Francis Group, an **informa** business

First edition published 2024
by CRC Press
4 Park Square, Milton Park, Abingdon, Oxon, OX14 4RN

and by CRC Press
6000 Broken Sound Parkway NW, Suite 300, Boca Raton, FL 33487-2742

CRC Press is an imprint of Informa UK Limited

British Library Cataloguing-in-Publication Data
A catalogue record for this book is available from the British Library

Library of Congress Cataloging-in-Publication Data
Names: Dadashi, Nastaran, author
Title: Intelligent infrastructure: user-centred remote condition monitoring / Nastaran Dadashi, David Golightly, Sarah Sharples, Richard Bye.
Description: First edition. | Boca Raton : CRC Press, [2023] | Includes bibliographical references and index.
Identifiers: LCCN 2022061396 (print) | LCCN 2022061397 (ebook) | ISBN 9781472471444 (hbk) | ISBN 9781032521169 (pbk) | ISBN 9781315587288 (ebk)
Subjects: LCSH: Structural health monitoring. | Structural failures--Prevention. | Infrastructure (Economics) | Remote sensing. | Detectors. | Public works--Protection.
Classification: LCC TA656.6 .D33 2023 (print) | LCC TA656.6 (ebook) | DDC 621.36/78--dc23/eng/20230208
LC record available at https://lccn.loc.gov/2022061396 LC ebook record available at https://lccn.loc.gov/2022061397

ISBN: 978-1-472-47144-4 (hbk)
ISBN: 978-1-032-52116-9 (pbk)
ISBN: 978-1-315-58728-8 (ebk)

DOI: 10.1201/9781315587288

Typeset in Times
by Deanta Global Publishing Services, Chennai, India

Contents

Foreword

The discipline of Human Factors has at its heart the incorporation of the understanding of the capabilities and limitations of people in designing complex systems. Complex infrastructures, such as those which enable our railways, roads, manufacturing industries, or logistics operations, often require vast, fixed assets, often over a wide geographical scale. These fixed assets have a limited lifespan, contain embedded carbon, and represent significant financial costs. Therefore, any technologies or systems which enable the proactive, efficient, and effective maintenance of these assets will deliver long-term economic benefits.

However, the nature of fixed infrastructures has undergone a step change in the past decades. Whereas once the infrastructures were dominated by the physical – bridges, roads, rails; and the mechanical – points or cranes; we now see an ever-increasing role for the digital. This presents tremendous opportunities, enabling a move from reactive or planned maintenance to proactive prediction of where intervention is required, and for the feasibility of data integration, enabling a whole systems view to be presented to and understood by operators. This results in a complex, multi-agent, socio-technical system. In addition, often, such systems have evolved through a principle of availability – where a technological breakthrough has made it possible to obtain and represent additional data from the system, it has been added. This results in a system that combines novel information with that obtained from legacy systems, and with gaps. The phrase "data, data, everywhere" comes to mind.

It has been long established that placing the user at the heart of design will result in more effective outcomes – better decision-making, increased engagement and situation awareness, and less need for re-work or post-hoc adjustments to designs. When considering Intelligent Infrastructure, users may vary in their roles, from onsite engineers, to remote system controllers, and to managers and policymakers. All may have different needs for the representation of information, at different levels of complexity and granularity.

This book proposes an approach which is "intelligence-led". We recognise the challenge presented by an evolving, complex, emergent system through a set of explorations of these complex systems, mainly in the rail context. The examples in this book consider a range of challenges. For example, the monitoring of ageing, heritage infrastructure can benefit from advanced sensing approaches, using both embedded sensing technologies and external high-accuracy observation tools. In new buildings or infrastructure, we can embed sensing as we are constructing, aiding the construction process itself. There is also an increasing capacity to monitor and control mechanical systems, such as points, robotics, or logistics technologies. When we start to move towards integrated, real-time systems that enable both monitoring and control, we can describe these systems as "digital twins".

We then propose approaches that consider how we can have appropriate frameworks and design solutions that start with the problem and the challenge and identify what decisions are being made, what the cognitive requirements are for a task, and what the goals of that task will be. The framework builds on a combination of learnings from the cases presented in this book, as well as an established theoretical understanding of design for automation and cognitive work. The aim of the framework is to help designers, developers, and human factors specialists in recognising the complexity of complex, distributed, Intelligent Infrastructure systems, and to shift thinking from "what data are available and how can we integrate and use these data" to "what do we need to understand in order to reach our goals more effectively, how can data help, and how do we select, combine and present those data to help"?

A whole systems approach is key to this thinking. Too often we can be seduced by technology, or we can see the people as the "weak links" in a complex system. The thinking that underpins this book recognises the role of partnership – the importance of an integrated consideration of how people, technologies, and infrastructure combine to achieve a common goal. The presence and proliferation of technology within what were previously physical systems will continue to increase. The examples in this book help on a pathway towards a new way of thinking, towards integrating our consideration of the physical, the digital, and people. We hope that readers enjoy the examples and approaches presented in this book. As we see the evolution of systems and data, it would be heartening to think that, alongside this, we can see a revolution in thinking, and the successful embedding of an intelligence-led approach to system development and design.

Sarah Sharples
October 2022.

About the Authors

Dr Nastaran Dadashi is Researcher, Educator, and a Chartered Human Factors Specialist. She has a PhD in Human Factors (Future Railway Intelligent Infrastructure) from the University of Nottingham, UK (Human Factors Research Group), where she worked as a research fellow. As a researcher, she applies human factors principles to a broad range of industries, including nuclear, health care, and the creative sector. As an educator, Nastaran works with digital experience designers at George Brown College, Canada (School of Design), to ensure that the next generation of digital innovations is accessible, ethical, and responsible.

Dr David Golightly is Lecturer in Human-Systems Integration within the Future Mobility Group at the School of Engineering, Newcastle University, UK. David is a Chartered Psychologist and Chartered Ergonomist, researching user-centred design for transport innovation and operations. This has included application of knowledge elicitation from experts for rail socio-technical systems modelling and in the human aspects of operational safety and performance for transport systems. David has also applied knowledge elicitation and decision-making analyses in support accident and incident investigation for manufacturing and in hospital care co-ordination. Prior to his research career, David led commercial usability and user-centred design programmes at a global telecoms provider and an FTSE100 fintech provider.

Professor Sarah Sharples is Professor of Human Factors at the University of Nottingham, UK. From 2015 to 2016, she was President of the Chartered Institute of Ergonomics and Human Factors. She is co-editor of the Ergonomics and Human Factors textbook *Evaluation of Human Work*: 4th edition. In 2021, she was appointed as Chief Scientific Adviser to the Department for Transport.

Richard Bye is Head of Ergonomics and Human Factors at Network Rail. Richard has been involved in a wide range of physical, cognitive and organisational ergonomics projects, working on initiatives as diverse as the assurance of safety-critical operational processes, the introduction of smartphones and tablets for frontline track workers, the development of decision support tools for the railway's internet of things, and the implementation of new technology to increase the resilience of real-time rail operations.

1 Introducing Human Factors for Remote Condition Monitoring

1.1 CHAPTER OVERVIEW

This chapter aims to set out the motivation and structure of the book, setting the scene for the work that is to follow. This includes:

- Introducing the context for the book – infrastructure monitoring
- Describing the importance of a human factors approach
- Setting out who should read the book and what is covered in the remaining chapters

1.2 THE MOTIVATION FOR THE BOOK

With the development of sensor technology, wireless communications, big data, and machine learning, there is an increasing interest in technologies and solutions that assess and predict the state of equipment and assets within various industrial settings. These technologies aim to collect information from multiple sources about infrastructure asset status. Then, through current and historical data analysis, this configuration of technologies delivers intelligence on current and future asset status to a maintenance operator or manager to inform optimal maintenance decision-making. These technologies are known under different terms – remote condition monitoring, e-maintenance, prognostic systems, predictive maintenance, and smart or Intelligent Infrastructure.

This approach is viewed as vital to the operation of large-scale systems such as transport infrastructure, utilities, manufacturing, process industries, hospitals, smart cities, oil, gas, and offshore renewable installations (e.g., Petkov, Wu, and Powell, 2020; Mikkonen and Lahdelma, 2014). In many respects, though, the capabilities and challenges discussed in this book are just as relevant to smaller, local forms of assets and asset systems, such as domestic appliance monitoring, as they are to major, strategic, and national infrastructure.

Let us take a context like the railways, the key motivating setting for the work that inspired this book. Remote condition monitoring is used to monitor and ideally predict the current and future state of a whole range of assets, including points, signals, earthworks, tunnels (including pumps that keep tunnels clear and

DOI: 10.1201/9781315587288-1

dry), bridges, passenger escalators, lifts, and ticket machines (e.g., Jing et al., 2021; Vinberg et al., 2018; Balouchi, Bevan and Formston, 2021). In addition, train-borne technologies can monitor both the train and the track it travels upon. Condition monitoring is an important technology in making rail operations more reliable and cost-effective, ultimately helping to deliver better value and better service to passengers and freight customers (Grubic, 2018; Bernal, Spiryagin, and Cole, 2018). Many rail assets are also safety critical, and ensuring they are functioning correctly is, therefore, important to ensure the health of the asset and the safety of the rail service. Predictive systems can also help extend the life of assets where they might be prohibitively expensive to replace (e.g., major civil engineering structures such as bridges and tunnels). Finally, maintenance and inspection of track and equipment are expensive and potentially dangerous, requiring staff to go out at night, to remote locations, or work around moving trains (Golightly et al., 2013). Reducing the need for staff to be present, or to maintain assets unnecessarily, can help keep them safe.

This approach is just as relevant to other forms of infrastructure. For example, Baah et al. (2015) present a risk-based approach to sanitary sewer pipe asset management, including a pipe condition grade prediction model, assessment of the consequence of failure, and risk of failure. The synthesised information can consequently inform future sewer pipe maintenance programmes. In this way, waste collection systems and technologies to facilitate monitoring the condition of wastewater can support better water management and prevent sewer-related groundwater contamination incidents.

Despite the promise of remote condition monitoring and predictive technologies, there is a growing concern with such technologies because they can be difficult or impractical to use. Operational staff may face huge volumes of data, which is in a relatively raw form, presenting problems of interpretation and information overload (Dadashi, Golightly, and Sharples 2017; Dorgo et al., 2018). Alarms may be complex to interpret and duplicated many times. At the other extreme, the outputs are simplified down to a simple "red-amber-green" alert with little explanation, where the reasoning of algorithms may be very unclear, or there may be reliability problems.

While the shift from regular to predictive maintenance can save money through a reduction in the need for visual inspection of assets, it requires operational staff to have trust in the algorithms that are helping them to make decisions and, potentially, to fundamentally change working practices that have been laid down for decades (Ciocoiu et al., 2017; Kefalidou et al., 2018). Furthermore, there are challenges due to the ongoing need for calibration. Once a system is installed, it is a new job to maintain the calibration of existing sensors, react to changes on the ground that may change what is being measured, and integrate new data sources so that the whole picture remains coherent. This needs ongoing resource and knowledge management (Golightly et al., 2018). In addition, the introduction of change in many industries requires leadership, guidance, and, most critically, a sociotechnical system view of change (Trist, 1981; Ottens et al., 2006 Wilson, 2014), where technology, people, and organisational structures (including processes) are viewed as interdependent. All of these challenges can be thought of as human factors challenges.

This book considers, in depth, the challenges placed on users of current and future condition monitoring systems. Its primary focus is to understand the cognitive processes, including managing alarms, interpreting data, and collaborating with automation, if we are to design technologies that support, rather than hinder, operational users. The book describes a range of human factors methods that can be used to understand the current and future functioning of people and technology in an enhanced maintenance and asset monitoring context. The book also presents a framework for describing these issues systematically and presents the resulting design considerations to increase the effectiveness of individual operators and organisations as a whole.

EXPLAINING THE TITLE – FROM INTELLIGENCE TO DATA

When thinking about remote condition monitoring, it is typical to focus first on an asset – normally vital, prone to failure, or both, such as an ageing suspension bridge (see Figure 1.1) For example, Ko and Ni (2005) present examples of the breadth of bridges' technologies for structural health monitoring systems, including sensing, communication, signal processing, data management, and information technology. The next step is to identify the data that can be generated (e.g., vibrations, temperature, wind speeds). Various hardware and software processes are applied (e.g., algorithms to interpret signals from accelerometers), partly to interpret the raw data but often to manage the sheer complexity of incoming data (e.g., from tens or hundreds of accelerometers on each cable of the bridge). Other data may be coupled with this analysis to give it "context" (e.g., traffic volumes). The results are then presented to an operator, hoping they will benefit their decision-making.

FIGURE 1.1   Golden Gate Bridge, San Francisco, USA (left) and First Forth Road Bridge, Scotland

This approach typically assumes a flow from "data" to "information", which is then used to inform decision-making or "knowledge". This kind of definition is found in ISO13774-4: 2015 for predictive maintenance, for example, and was the approach adopted in the data to intelligence (D2I) framework (Dadashi et al., 2014), developed at an early stage of our work.

The rest of this book argues that this approach is flawed: specifically, that it is back-to-front. This book argues that if the goal is to develop a user-centred technology that fits well with current and future operator needs and abilities, the process must start by considering what is intelligence for infrastructure management. What do people do? How do they make decisions? Importantly, this is not just one decision, but multiple decisions made by different individuals and groups, who are separated both in time and space – sometimes at the same time, sometimes under time pressure. What are their aims when making these decisions? What are their strategies, perceptions, and assumptions – both correct and incorrect? From this starting point, we can see that the information will be needed to support these current or, maybe, improved decisions and outcomes. Understanding the information and how it is used makes us to understand what analysis is needed to provide information and, critically, to determine when the analysis, particularly with automation, needs to be a collaborative effort between technology and human expertise. It is only then that the correct data can be selected for sensing. Putting this slightly differently, rather than working from what data we *can* collect and thinking about how that can be integrated and synthesised to inform intelligence, we think about what intelligence we need, and, by modelling the data requirements that flow from this decision-making need, we can identify the best way to develop an Intelligent Infrastructure system.

In practice, it might be that both approaches ("data to intelligence" and "intelligence to data") play a role – see Figure 1.2. The motivation for this book is to both show that there is a vital role for the "intelligence to data" path and act as a guide to following this path.

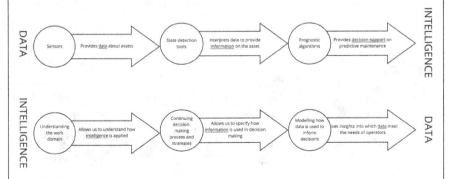

FIGURE 1.2 Contrasting from data to intelligence with from intelligence to data

1.3 MONITORING AND PREDICTING ASSET PERFORMANCE

Much of our infrastructure is ageing. Mynatt et al. (2017) reported that America's infrastructure (i.e., civil engineering) needs $3.9 trillion in new investment. The solution is not only to replace and enhance existing physical infrastructure but also to optimise its lifespan with smart technologies that can communicate their own state.

Unprecedented climate change implications further emphasise the benefit of real-time data collection and analysis. Assets are more susceptible to extreme events such as flooding and therefore need close attention. Also, the erosive effects of more extreme climate mean historically effective cycles for maintenance may no longer apply. Asset monitoring and prediction can provide the means to fill this information gap.

Technologies range from simple condition monitoring devices with basic recognition of the system status to highly intelligent and connected sensors coupled with predictive algorithms to provide an overall understanding of the asset now and, crucially, its state, behaviour, or response in the short-term and long-term future. Recent technological and organisational advances have increased the potential for automated, remote monitoring and predictive fault diagnosis of infrastructure assets. Examples include supporting predictive maintenance of a ship using onboard measurements (Liu et al., 2022) or monitoring a pumping station to optimise maintenance and enhance flood defence assets (Tarrant et al., 2018). This configuration of technologies, sometimes referred to as predictive maintenance or "Intelligent Infrastructure", is being realised in various domains and sectors, including water and sewage, oil and gas, and transport.

With the advent of very cheap and reliable electronic devices and sensors, the notion of big data driving asset sensing and monitoring has become more of a reality. This enables the generation of immediate, accurate, and relevant information about the state of the infrastructure, as well as enhancing safety and efficiency through optimising the use of the infrastructure. There are, therefore, many potential benefits:

- **Better data about asset behaviour and performance** – at its core, these technologies are about sensing the state of an asset. State information may include material properties, environmental conditions, location, or a detailed record of the movement of parts. New sensing and data collection technology mean this data can be captured continuously with greater fidelity than ever before, with multiple, accurate sensors. Not only can this sense the state of the asset now, but it also supports an emerging picture over time. The ability to measure multiple assets consistently means that deviations from the norm can be seen either in an individual asset or potentially regarding a whole suite of assets (e.g., across an entire estate of buildings using the same air conditioning unit). This, coupled with machine learning, enables learning about the behaviour of a whole class of assets in an extensive range of different settings, which can inform not only maintenance but the future design of products and technologies.

- **Beyond human sensing** – sometimes, sensors can pick up change that is beyond human perception. This may be because the changes are too fast, such as technologies that monitor changes within explosive blasts. Others can monitor changes that are too slow – the kind of creep and degradation of metal in a steel structure may not be visible to the human eye. Finally, changes may be too small. Acoustic monitoring systems can pick up breaks in suspension bridge cables that would be inaudible to the human ear (Li and He, 2012).
- **Predictive maintenance** – historically, maintenance is conducted at regular intervals (Jang and Lee, 2017). These intervals may be based on experience. While this experience is often appropriate, it can also be out-of-date with new, more reliable assets or new patterns of operational use (Garcia Marquez, 2007) (e.g., track points that were once used daily are now only used very occasionally). Predictive maintenance allows an asset operator to plan an inspection, maintenance, and renewals based on accurate predictions of the future state of the asset (Ghofrani, 2020). This means assets can be replaced before they fail, but it also means that assets can be left in place rather than being replaced on a fixed schedule, or suites of assets can be replaced or repaired at a time that gives the best efficiency or economy of scale.
- **Better operational continuity** – ultimately, the gain is better operational continuity. First, assets can be repaired or replaced before they fail, and second, repairs or replacements can be scheduled to cause minimum disruption. In an environment like the railway, this can mean better planning renewals and inspections while ensuring that there is continuous service as best as possible. This is critical for a system like the railways, where disruption is the most significant cause of passenger dissatisfaction (Kurup et al., 2021) and a source of substantial lost revenue (NAO, 2008).
- **Reduced exposure for staff** – in some cases, sensors can be put in places where it is simply not possible or safe for humans to access (e.g., within running machinery, high-hazard areas such as nuclear reactors or chemical processing). In other cases, this can remove the need for people to go to dangerous or remote locations (e.g., on railway tracks, on highways, or offshore installations).
- **Reduced waste** – infrastructure companies currently inspect (and sometimes replace) assets whether they actually need them or not. This is an expensive, inefficient, and non-sustainable use of resources. This is not just replacing assets but oiling, testing, and maintaining assets when the state of the asset does not demand it. The cost of wasted effort is significant; predictive technologies should help to fix this.
- **Servitisation of asset management and maintenance** – the ability to monitor and manage asset status is moving producers from being providers of products to providers of services. Typified in the 1990s by the Rolls-Royce Aerospace "Power by the Hour" philosophy (Smith, 2013), manufacturers can not only monitor their assets in operations, but they can also organise

maintenance and advise on use. In addition, manufacturers can refine their own designs and products and plan new products based on knowledge of actual product use and performance. The aim is to move from find and fix (maintenance as a job) to monitor and manage (reliability as a service). This can and should be a significant change in how organisations, and a maintenance supply chain ensure the cost-effective availability of assets.

We explore asset technologies in more detail in Chapter 2, providing examples, potential challenges, and opportunities.

1.4 THE HUMAN FACTORS CHALLENGE

The introduction of highly reliable sensors and remote condition monitoring equipment will change the form and functionality of maintenance and engineering systems within many infrastructure sectors. Process, transport, and infrastructure companies are increasingly looking to remote condition monitoring to increase reliability and decrease costs in the future. However, while many of the technical challenges of designing such systems are already known (Aktan et al., 1998), such systems will present human factors challenges.

Human factors, or ergonomics, study and apply methods and processes to understand how people work together and they would interact with technology within systems (Wilson and Sharples, 2015). Originally orientated towards the primarily physical aspects of work, this discipline has increasingly looked to understanding the cognitive and organisational aspects of work. This includes how people learn, solve problems, and make decisions and how this is influenced by the design and structure of work, including the culture of an organisation. Also, the emphasis has moved from purely work systems to understand more about consumer products or public service design (the design of buses, stations, aeroplanes, and buildings). In return, human factors have adopted many of the approaches from allied disciplines in human–computer interaction, psychology, physiology, design, user experience (UX), and sociology.

Human factors has at its heart a systems approach, recognising the interaction between multiple people, technologies, and artefacts in a setting, considering not only the design of a specific work environment or task, but the wider organisational, societal, economic, regulatory, and legal setting (Rasmussen, 1997; Wilson and Sharples, 2015). A helpful way of summarising the impact of human factors can be to recognise that humans have capabilities and limitations – the job of integrated human factors is to minimise the negative impact of human limitations and maximise human capabilities (see Figure 1.3).

Little is expressed about information presentation requirements within the relevant standards and guidelines in considering the human factors of asset monitoring and predictive maintenance (e.g., ISO13374). Clearly, there is a danger that different personnel using such technologies in different functions and for different purposes could be swamped by the sheer quantity of information provided for them, without any filtering, or else they are provided with information more suited to another job function

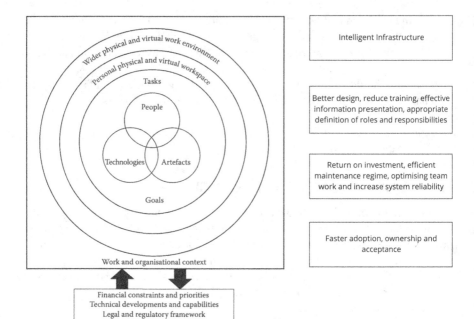

FIGURE 1.3   Sociotechnical systems model

with different goals. This is particularly the case when technologies involve a high degree of automation. Poorly designed automation can lead to confusion, a lack of trust, over-reliance on technology, and degradation of skills (Bainbridge, 1983).

There is a need to ensure that any asset monitoring or predictive technology is designed and deployed to meet the needs, capabilities, and limitations of the people who are intended to use and benefit. Many successful implementations exist, many with good interface design and strong design and deployment rationale (Golightly et al., 2018), but little systematic analysis across the paradigm. Furthermore, many implementations fail, and it is acknowledged that a crucial part of this is the poor match between technology design and the actual patterns of usage that operators need to adopt (Golightly et al., 2018; Kefalidou et al., 2018). For every success story, there are anecdotes of operators being overwhelmed and confused, not trusting technology, and ultimately rejecting the new ways of working.

One of the fundamental principles of a human factors approach is the principle of user-centred design (ISO 9241-210 [ISO, 2010]) (see Figure 1.4).

User-centred design advocates the representation and, wherever possible, the active participation of intended users at every stage of the design process. Methods from human factors are often about capturing what users do, how they perceive their activity, or about representing this for others to understand and apply (e.g., in software design). Central to this is the idea of understanding the context of work, or "Work as Done" (in contrast to "Work as Imagined" by senior management, software

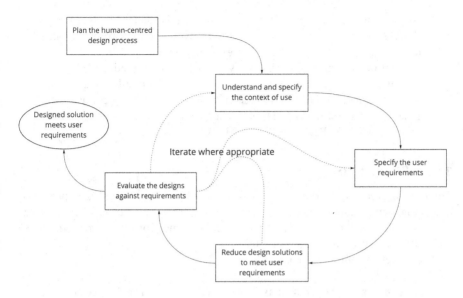

FIGURE 1.4 User-centred design process as described in human-centred design activities (ISO 9241-210, 2010)

developers, or project managers) (Hollnagel, 2017). In this book, our main aim is to understand the context of work and "Work as Done" in asset monitoring situations, using rail as a case in point.

The overall benefits of taking a human factors, user-centred approach are:

- **Better designs** – by taking a user-centred approach, the design of technology (or training programmes or processes) will be better fitted to people's needs, abilities, and limitations. The outcomes are better performance, greater user satisfaction, increased safety (for the user and safety-critical tasks, for the whole system), and user well-being.
- **Reduced training, faster adoption** – for work-related technologies, taking a user-centred approach and following ergonomics design principles can also make the technology easier to learn. In an environment such as Intelligent Infrastructure, this does not just mean overly simplified, but rather that the design meets the user's expectations and pre-existing knowledge. This can reduce training and adoption times.
- **Ownership and acceptance** – the philosophy of actively engaging users *from the outset* means that users feel like they have been actively considered as part of the development process. They feel greater ownership and commitment to the project and act as advocates to other user communities.
- **De-risking the design process** – one of the common problems with software design and deployment is to find substantial barriers to adoption late in the design process or, worse, after the technology has been procured. In

software development and procurement costs, this can lead to expensive re-designs and change requests. By actively involving users from the outset, technologies and processes can be designed right the first time.

- **Return on investment** – Ultimately, the benefits outlined above in terms of better performance, reduced training, faster adoption leading to seeing the anticipated benefits, and de-risking of the design process are a cost-effective pursuit. Money and time spent on engaging users can pay for itself many times over (Pew and Mavor, 2007).

1.5   ABOUT THIS BOOK

The overall aim of this book is to demonstrate why human factors is important to asset monitoring context and illustrate the methods that can be used to better understand how asset technologies and remote condition monitoring can meet the needs and abilities of its current and future users.

The objectives of this book are:

- **To provide an overview of asset monitoring systems** (Chapter 2) – introduce remote condition monitoring systems and their characteristics and applications as well as existing and future challenges of emerging, more intelligent technologies, such as predictive maintenance or Intelligent Infrastructure.
- **To introduce human factors for asset monitoring systems** (Chapter 3) – to set out the major concerns and considerations that need to be taken on-board to understand a user of remote condition monitoring solutions in their various forms. This includes some of the core ideas of human factors theory, such as how people work with supervisory control systems.
- **To describe the relevant methods of human factors** (Chapter 4) – understanding complex control environments, in order to inform design, requires methods that capture and represent the important characteristics of complex work. The book will introduce a number of these methods that can be used in combination.
- **To understand cognitive work in asset monitoring contexts** (Chapters 5–7) – to design for these kinds of systems and environments, we need to fully understand the context of deployment – this is both in terms of the work environment and in terms of tasks and cognitive activities. These chapters present two relevant environments – maintenance monitoring and electrical control, to consider issues such as coping strategies with different levels of information and automation and for managing asset alarms.
- **To introduce a framework of the railway, focusing on the data processing required to enable informed and improved decision-making** (Chapter 8) – to present an interview study that was aimed to understand Intelligent Infrastructure within the railway, understand and explore the

range of human factors issues, and develop insights with regards to data processing activities within Intelligent Infrastructure.

- **To produce guidance for future development and implementation of Intelligent Infrastructure systems in the railway, which will match and complement human capabilities and needs** (Chapter 9) – this guidance, informed by the data processing framework, had two purposes: firstly, it assists in designing and developing future Intelligent Infrastructure. Secondly, the methodological approach adopted and practised in this book provides guidance to human factors specialists in exploring cognition in complex sociotechnical systems. Furthermore, applications of these recommendations were used to explore Intelligent Infrastructure within other sectors.

1.6 INTENDED AUDIENCE FOR THIS BOOK

While based on rail, this book is intended to highlight the importance of human factors to many applications of Intelligent Infrastructure. We also hope to convey the use of certain methods and approaches that support understanding the design and deployment of remote condition monitoring. Therefore, we hope this book will be of most benefit to:

- **Designers and developers** of remote condition monitoring and predictive maintenance solutions who wish to know more about getting the best out of their systems – how to make them more usable and, through a user-centred design approach, de-risk the development process. These could be from any remote condition monitoring environment, so we spend some time describing the rail environment so that readers can draw parallels with their own specific domains. Also, these could come from any part of the supply chain – Original Equipment Manufacturers (OEMs) supplying the asset, providers of condition monitoring and predictive maintenance solutions, and systems integration providers.
- **Managers of infrastructure environments** – these could be people in an operational context seeking to understand the issues that operators face or those involved in the procurement of solutions looking to find appropriate user-centred technologies.
- **Rail engineers** – people with specific rail knowledge wishing to understand more about the implications and human aspects of rail maintenance and new technologies.
- **Policymakers and funders** – this includes regulators, funders, researchers, and innovation incubators. Many of these organisations are spending or offering significant sums of money to make a case for predictive maintenance, complete R&D, and get early products to market. Knowing what good looks, particularly from an end-user perspective, can increase the chance of product success.

- **Human factors practitioners and researchers** moving into remote condition monitoring design and wishing to know more about the challenges involved. This may include students, probably at a post-graduate level.

1.7 CHAPTER SUMMARY

Having set out the aims and structure of this book, Chapter 2 presents detail on remote condition monitoring concepts. It also gives more information on the rail context that underpinned the case studies used in this book.

2 Remote Condition Monitoring and Predictive Maintenance

2.1 CHAPTER OVERVIEW

Chapter 1 introduced the motivation and structure of the book. This chapter aims to give a more detailed introduction to remote condition monitoring, particularly for people new to the domain (e.g., human factors specialists who are new to maintenance technologies). This includes:

- Providing a definition and description of remote condition monitoring
- Providing detail on the rail context, which serves as the case study domain for this book
- Introducing the lack of understanding of human aspects of predictive maintenance and infrastructure management

2.2 DEFINING REMOTE CONDITION MONITORING

A shortage in infrastructural resources is coupled with growing demand for capacity (Crainic et al., 2009). Due to space, materials, and resource constraints, building new infrastructure to fulfil capacity demands is no longer always an option. Additionally, the development of new infrastructure can be particularly challenging in dense, urban environments.

Therefore, a more optimal approach to infrastructure management is necessary to enable existing infrastructure to respond to increasing capacity demands. This is made possible with recent technological and organisational advances. Reliable sensors, sophisticated algorithms, and advanced surveillance systems have enabled proactive monitoring of infrastructure systems to ensure their reliability and availability to support the demands placed upon them. Table 2.1 covers the basic elements of a remote condition monitoring implementation.

A review of the literature on predictive maintenance systems in various domains (Adriaens et al., 2003; Aktan et al., 1998; Schrom et al., 2017; Tokody et al., 2018; Diyan et al., 2020) confirms that although these systems differ in terms of components and complexity, there are commonalities in terms of their high-level functions, principles that they aim to achieve, and overall service optimisation. In a report

DOI: 10.1201/9781315587288-2

TABLE 2.1

Basic Elements of Implementing Remote Condition Monitoring

Element	Description
Data collection	Collecting raw data from assets through sensors and tracking technologies
Intelligent analysis	Systems that integrate raw data and provide insight into the asset performance and its health condition
Access and presentation	Visualise and present the health condition to respective operators and decision-makers
Key performance indicators	Ensure that health conditions are effectively monitored and facilitate a proactive maintenance regime
Connections	Reliable data distribution and management (e.g., phone network, hard-wired, 5G)

published by the Royal Academy of Engineering in 2012 (RAE, 2012), four key principles are mentioned:

- Data: turned into information, into knowledge, and then into value
- Analysis: synthesising and interpretation, based on specific contextual needs
- Feedback: learning from experience and enhancing its effectiveness
- Adaptability: adaptive, resilient, and, consequently, sustainable infrastructure

Important data properties can include accuracy, integrity, completeness, consistency, and continuity between different assets and settings. Traceability, history, lifecycle, and verifiability give confidence in the data, but availability and accessibility are also required to get the data to the intended users (or sub-systems).

Another perspective is offered by Aktan et al. (1998), who conducted a series of studies to develop a remote condition monitoring-enabled system to support civil infrastructure monitoring. They defined stages/phases of infrastructure management as:

- Sense the definitive features of the piece of infrastructure.
- Reason the condition by analysing the information captured and performance criteria.
- Communicate the findings through appropriate interfaces.
- Learn from infrastructure condition patterns.
- Decide the optimum course of action.

In other words, condition monitoring aims to centralise data from existing technologies and analyse it before presenting it to the operator in an appropriate format that can directly assist them with the decision-making problem at hand. Often, this is used in a comparison or combination with historical data and involves predicting asset state. In the most advanced conceptions, it may offer actual maintenance advice and plans, though there are few practical examples.

Going beyond simply sensing and interpreting the current state of an asset, predictive and proactive maintenance can be defined as "the deep embedding of sensing, computing, and communication capabilities into traditional urban and rural physical infrastructure ... for the purpose of increasing efficiency, resiliency, and safety" (Mynatt et al., 2017). This supports a service that enables evidence-based operations and decision-making in a way that it is:

- Descriptive: accurate and timely characterisation of the current state
- Prescriptive: recommends immediate and near-term actions
- Predictive: anticipates future challenges and opportunities
- Planful: guides complex decision-making and scenario planning

Remote condition monitoring could be seen as a fitting technology to infrastructure, but it is much more complex than that. It is a holistic approach to modelling and managing complex infrastructure systems (Josey, 2013), requiring raw asset data, data analytics, asset optimisation, and knowledge management. Interconnectivity and the need for transparent and accurate data/information/ knowledge communication are essential attributes of effective infrastructure management. They may involve compatibility and integration, often with third-party assets and legacy technology. Getting this legacy integration right can cause significant challenges for successful implementation (Kefalidou et al., 2018).

2.3 APPLICATIONS OF PREDICTIVE MAINTENANCE

Various domains and industrial sectors have benefited/have the potential to benefit from remote condition monitoring. ISO/IEC TR 22417:2017: information technology – internet of things (IoT) – use cases include use cases such as transport infrastructure, home, public buildings, agriculture, and smart cities, to name only a few. Figure 2.1 gives an example of a cleaning machine. Other examples include energy (Coble et al., 2015; Sheng, 2017; Costello et al., 2017; Ramchurn et al., 2012; Akhondi et al., 2010), manufacturing (Lau et al., 2002), undersea and petro-chemical (Strasunskas, 2006), space exploration (Park et al., 2006), civil infrastructure (Aktan et al., 1998, 2000), water and sewage (Adriaens et al., 2003), defence (Jones et al., 1581998), and, the critical domain for this book, transportation (e.g., Ollier, 2006; Khan, 2007; Durazo-Cardenas et al., 2018; Vileiniskis et al., 2016; Armstrong and Preston, 2020; Vaghefi et al., 2012; Whelan et al., 2009; Koenig et al., 2019). Table 2.2 describes how the attributes of predictive maintenance apply to a selection of different domains.

2.3.1 AN EXAMPLE: REMOTE CONDITION MONITORING FOR DECARBONISATION

Climate change and reducing carbon output is the critical challenge of our time. We can see the potential application of remote condition monitoring within the energy sector, facilitating optimisation in multiple ways. First, it can be used for health monitoring of hard-to-access components such as reactor vessels or offshore wind

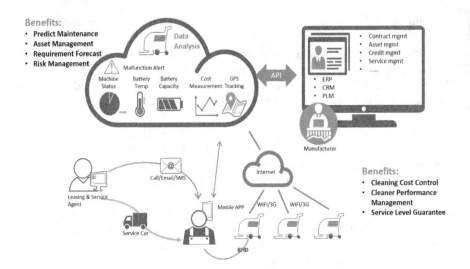

FIGURE 2.1 IoT application for cleaning machine leasing– (taken from ISO/IEC TR 22417:2017).

turbine arrays and, consequently, to increase the efficiency of power plants (e.g., Coble et al., 2015; Sheng, 2017; Costello et al., 2017; Ramchurn et al., 2012). In addition, connected sensors can provide the basis to explore the environmental benefits for the environment of plants and processes associated with energy harvesting. One crucial need for efficient and accurate health monitoring systems within the energy sector is due to recent licence extensions. In the USA, 74 reactors have been approved for first-round licence extensions (beyond 60 years), and therefore, real-time monitoring of the health of a wide range of components within power plants is essential (Coble et al., 2015).

Also, a wide range of research studies has explored the capability and connectivity of sensor-enabled networks (e.g., Akhondi et al., 2010). These capabilities have provided opportunities to develop smart energy management capabilities for both power suppliers and consumers. For example, McRoberts (2018) introduces a unified infrastructure that intelligently manages packaged power within the mining industry that is more resilient to outages and component failures.

A key contributor to creating a low-carbon built environment will be the integration of smart building systems. These systems improve asset reliability and performance, reducing energy use, optimising how space is used, and minimising the environmental impact of the buildings. For example, Creative Energy Homes is a seven-house development at the University of Nottingham that provides living test sites to inform the integration of energy-efficient technologies into housing (see Figure 2.2). The building will turn into a living organism: networked, intelligent, flexible, sensitive, and adaptable. Examples include Mogles et al. (2017), who present smarter, building-aware, and more personalised, digital energy feedback.

TABLE 2.2

The Potential of Predictive Maintenance and Remote Condition Monitoring across Multiple Domains

	Descriptive	Prescriptive	Predictive	Proactive
Intelligent transportation	Real-time traffic congestion information	Reroute traffic; adjust dynamic lane configuration (direction)	Anticipate rush hour/large event congestion; anticipate weather-related accidents	Suggest traffic patterns w/ intelligent stoplights
Intelligent energy management	Real-time energy demand information	Improve asset utilisation and management across transmission and distribution system	Anticipate the demand response required to ensure grid reliability	Suggest new market approaches to integrate production and distribution capabilities
Intelligent public safety and security	Real-time crowd analysis	Threat detection; dispatch public safety officers	Anticipate vulnerable settings and events	Suggest new communication and coordination response approaches
Intelligent disaster response	Real-time water levels in flood-prone areas	Timely levee management and evacuations as needed	Anticipate flood inundation with low-cost digital terrain maps	Inform National Flood Insurance Programme; inform vulnerable populations
Intelligent city systems	Describe mobility patterns (pedestrian, cycling, automobile, trucking, electric, and autonomous vehicles)	Adjust mobility management to improve safety and reduce energy usage	Anticipate changing needs for parking, charging stations, bike, and ride share programmes	Inform future mobility capabilities to drive economic development and reduce barriers to employment
Intelligent agriculture	Characterise spatial and temporal variability in soil, crop, and weather	Advise based on environmental stressors and crop traits	Forecast crop yield; anticipate seasonal water needs	Customise management practices and seed selection to local conditions
Intelligent health	Block-level assessment of current allergens/air pollutant levels	Inform asthma action plans based on local conditions	Anticipate peak seasonal spikes in allergen and air pollutant levels	Inform transportation plans to shift road use away from "asthma corridors"

Source: Taken from Mynatt et al. (2017).

FIGURE 2.2   Exterior of the Nottingham House, Green Close, University Park (Nottingham, UK)

Having presented a general definition and purpose for remote condition monitoring and predictive maintenance, the chapter now covers the specifics of one domain – rail remote condition monitoring. The following section provides context to the case study domain described in the rest of the book and research conducted explicitly for the Great Britain rail infrastructure provider, Network Rail.

2.4   REMOTE CONDITION MONITORING FOR RAIL

Railways are typical of a domain increasingly adopting predictive monitoring and maintenance solutions as part of a wider move towards digitalisation. Using this domain as a point of discussion and analysis facilitates our conversation around the challenges of delivering user-centred remote condition monitoring and predictive maintenance. The description also helps to illustrate some of the major motivations for infrastructure management and some of the key challenges. Suppose we can tame predictive maintenance in a complex environment such as the railway. In that case, the chances are we can follow the same paradigm for other complex socio-technical environments.

2.4.1   MAINTAINING THE RAILWAYS

The issues we have discussed of increased demands on capacity, the need for continuous, cost-effective availability, and the requirement to be robust in the face of climate change are all relevant to the railways. In many parts of the world, demand for the rail system is at its highest and is only set to increase, with rail offering a low-carbon alternative for private cars, short-haul flights, and road freight. This book focuses on the rail system in Great Britain, but the challenges and solutions are just as relevant to rail globally (ERRAC, 2017; IEA, 2019). While we primarily discuss mainline rail, these issues covered are just as relevant to light and urban transit, which has a vital role in moving people in and around cities as urbanisation increases (UN, 2018).

Rail infrastructure requires maintenance to ensure continuous availability and safe performance. Track, overhead line equipment, and structures such as bridges, tunnels, and embankments require routine inspection. Much of the work, both inspection and maintenance, still relies on human effort. In 2012, an inspection of Great Britain's 16,000 km of track and 2560 stations required 1.3 million hours of work. While new technologies such as the Plain Line Pattern have improved that situation, staff still have a substantial physical need to go out on track. For example, during the 2019 Easter weekend, over 13,000 maintenance staff worked to build and repair Great Britain's rail infrastructure.

This work occurs in a potentially hazardous environment, where track workers need protection from nearby service or engineering trains. It can also occur in remote or difficult-to-access locations such as tunnels, at night, and in poor weather (Farrington-Darby et al., 2005; Schock et al., 2010; Golightly et al., 2013b). Inspection and maintenance require consistent, time-intensive, high-quality work from a skilled but ageing workforce and complex decision-making with an ever-increasing volume of asset data.

Failure to safely maintain the network can lead to significant delay and disruption (Szymula and Bešinović, 2020). Signal, track, and point failures are the most critical and difficult events to manage (Golightly and Dadashi, 2017). The initial steps associated with identifying and managing a fault are crucial (Belmonte et al., 2011). Failure to rapidly identify and diagnose a problem can lead to "out-of-control", unmanageable situations, and significant rail disruption. When failures occur during peak times at busy points in the network, the effects can be huge, with many tens of thousands of delayed passengers and significant damage to passenger confidence and the reputation of the railways.

More crucially, safety is the paramount concern for improving railway maintenance, and maintenance failures can impair the safety of the railways (Kim and Yoon, 2013). In practice, the railways in Great Britain (GB) and across the European Union (EU) have an exceptional safety record (ERRAC, 2017), but outcomes can be disastrous when failures occur.

As a case in point, a Virgin West Coast Pendolino service from London to Glasgow derailed on February 23, 2007, with one passenger fatality (RAIB, 2008). Deterioration of the point machines at Lambrigg was considered as being the immediate cause of the failure. This was due to (1) the mechanical failure of a bolted joint, (2) the incorrect setup of points, and (3) a track inspection that was missed on February 18, 2007 (RAIB, 2008). Although images taken previously with the New Measurement Train showed evidence of defects, the output did not lead to planned maintenance. In other words, while technology theoretically generates the required data, this only works if the required decision-making is in place. Accidents such as this, the accident at Potter's Bar in 2002, or Brétigny-sur-Orge in 2013, have fundamentally shaped how maintenance and inspection are conducted and organised. The need to strive for better performance is a constant aim of all rail stakeholders.

2.4.2 THE ROLE AND POTENTIAL FOR PROACTIVE MAINTENANCE

There is, therefore, a growing need to apply autonomous maintenance and inspection technologies to reduce physical exposure to hazards, improve the volume and speed of data collection and analysis, and offer the opportunity to release human expertise from physical labour for problem-solving and decision-making.

Currently, inspection is a combination of visual observation and the use of specialist recording and measurement tools. In some cases, the inspection is purely manual. People go out on track and check assets for their physical condition. In less accessible places, they may use Unmanned Aerial Vehicles (UAVs) for checking assets such as bridges. Furthermore, other roles may be involved in identifying failures. For example, a driver might report that a signal is malfunctioning. In other cases, data is collected about the assets but can only be accessed locally, with staff going out to a location and downloading relevant data (e.g., from the condition of a point) and bringing it back to the maintenance control room for additional review and assessment. If any abnormalities are observed, they plan the repairs. Otherwise, maintenance technicians located in control rooms will notice the failure and send the relevant track workers to fix the defect when an asset fails. Sometimes this is a full repair. In other cases, where there is only partial asset deterioration, an assessment is made, and a strategy is applied as to when the full repair should be made. For example, it might be more cost-effective to plan this in line with a more substantial infrastructure upgrade in the area or to assess whether a suite or fleet of assets is all due for replacement.

POINT CONDITION MONITORING

Point machines are an example of an asset where remote condition monitoring can play a key role. Point machines enable trains to switch from one track to another. Malfunction of points is costly and, more importantly, can cause accidents. The accident at Potters Bar in May 2002 (Health and Safety Executive, 2003) was a tragic case of a point failure that led to 7 fatalities and 76 injuries (Adetunji, 2011). Since monitoring and maintaining point machines are critical for the rail network, Point Condition Monitoring (PCM) equipment is used to facilitate this. PCM systems use trackside sensors and record the current flow in the point machines to determine whether they are in working condition or not (Garcia Marquez et al., 2007). A number of PCM systems are being used by Network Rail. Some are embedded within Fault Management Systems (FMS), while others are standalone point monitoring systems. These collections of RCM equipment facilitate a more efficient service through better

FIGURE 2.3   Picture of a point. Credit: Network Rail

reactive maintenance. This aims to integrate available data to allow for proactive and predictive maintenance. An example of a point is shown in Figure 2.3.

In order to collect reliable and timely information regarding the wide range of assets that are dispersed across the network nationwide, railway infrastructure has increasingly relied on the use of remote condition monitoring. This is a capability that enables the data collection from assets to identify functional failures. These systems collate the acquired data from sensors and loggers and present the appropriate information regarding the health status of the infrastructure to a control room operator. Remote condition monitoring provides a platform to collect, synthesise, and interpret data regarding individual assets and, in doing so, supports a human operator in programming the maintenance process in order to mitigate the risk of potential failures (Carretero et al., 2003).

Since these systems are costly to implement, it is important to carefully select and prioritise which assets are monitored with remote condition monitoring equipment. These are selected based on their safety criticality and the effect of their failure on the efficiency of the service (i.e., delays and track availability). Remote condition monitoring systems have been used on the rail network for many years. As early as 2006, Network Rail had 3000 remote condition monitoring systems across its infrastructure, monitoring a diverse range of asset types (e.g., signal, point machine, overhead lines) (Ollier, 2006).

Rail RCM are divided into two groups: train-borne RCM and trackside RCM. Train-borne RCM is facilitated by sensors installed on a train, while trackside RCM has been made possible with the help of sensors directly installed on the infrastructure (Bint, 2008). However, there is a crossover in that trackside sensing may monitor rolling stock (e.g., detecting wheel flats), and trains have the equipment to sense track conditions.

Proactive maintenance goes beyond this, and it is mainly considered in terms of centralising and integrating the support currently provided to infrastructure maintenance by monitoring the condition of assets remotely but providing greater levels of automation, interpretation, and integration of data sources. Potential failure or unnecessary fixed-term replacements will then be prevented by providing proactive information to the maintenance function. Currently, maintaining assets is done through fixed schedules. This approach is time-consuming and costly and involves risk both to staff required to go out on track and the potential risk of asset failure before a routine inspection picks up a fault. This routine inspection approach can be replaced by analysing real-time information regarding the assets and attending to the trackside equipment only when necessary. Most critically, however, it can predict if and when an asset is likely to fail, thus ensuring that it is repaired or replaced *before* it becomes an issue that impedes performance or impacts safety. Therefore, predictive and proactive maintenance in rail will move the railway, especially its maintenance and engineering activities, from "find and fix" mentality to "predict and prevent" and potentially to "design and prevent" (Bint, 2008). In Network Rail, as with several other settings, this kind of predictive maintenance is called "Intelligent Infrastructure".

2.5   CHALLENGES WITH DEPLOYING REMOTE CONDITION MONITORING

Section 2.3 introduced the basic process of remote condition monitoring, from raw data to information and storage. While this provides a valuable framework, it leaves a number of open questions – What is the context of use? What are the patterns that need to be recognised? Who will benefit? How will it be used? These questions are no different from what we would ask with other interactive products such as websites and mobile applications. However, they have been rarely explored to their full extent within types of remote condition monitoring projects. This is simply because the scope of predictive and proactive maintenance projects is often too broad. Designers and developers may be enthusiastic about how they add any available technology without an appreciation of its value and role to the overall design solution or as part of a broader set of tools applied by end-users (Golightly et al., 2018). This oversimplification or reductionist fallacy is common in more complex technology design and deployment (Feltovich et al., 2004).

There is a potential for standards to inform the design of such systems. ISO13374-1: condition monitoring and diagnostics of machines; data processing, communication, and presentations (Figure 2.4) is one such relevant standard. ISO13374-1 aims to provide the basic requirements for open software specifications, allowing machine condition monitoring data and information to be processed. ISO 13374-1 suggests six stages for data processing and information flow: data acquisition, data manipulation, state detection, health assessment, prognostic assessment, and advisory generation.

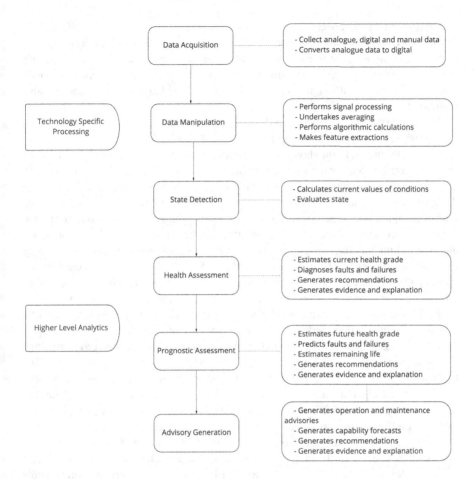

FIGURE 2.4 ISO 13374 strategic framework (taken from Network Rail, 2015).

In addition to standards that guide the design and development of RCMs, specific guidelines such as Engineering Equipment and Materials Users Association (EEMUA) 191 also exist to inform best practices for designing alarms, particularly alarm management systems. These guidelines inform effective alarm systems within industrial settings (e.g., chemical manufacture, power generation, oil, and gas) but may not be as effective or as easy to follow when incorporating "smart" technologies within more everyday socio-technical systems (e.g., smart home, health monitoring systems).

Standards and guidelines apply to specific safety-critical domains (e.g., nuclear industry NUREG-0711: Rev. 1 Human Factors Engineering Programme Review Model). As a highly regulated environment, control systems adopted within nuclear power plants, often equipped with a wide range of asset management technology, need to follow a specific range of standards and guidelines. These guidelines have led to the need for early design planning and early incorporation of human factors activities.

Finally, ISO11064 covers the design of control centres. Specifically, ISO 11064-4:2013 specifies ergonomic principles, recommendations, and requirements for workstations found in control centres. The standard covers control workstation's design, emphasising layout and dimensions, primarily for seated, visual display-based workstations, although control workstations at which operators stand are also addressed.

There are two major issues with design standards such as those described above. First, despite the standards and guidelines, there is very little (if any) guidance in terms of how information should be presented to users. For example, ISO 13374-1 explores communication and presentation but does not specifically guide how to achieve this from a user perspective. EEMUA 191 discusses best practices within designing alarm systems but does not explore data collection and analysis methods within complex socio-technical systems to choose the right alarm configurations. Also, as we cover later in the book, predictive maintenance systems may be as much about searching and interpreting information (user pull) as sending alerts and alarms to a user (system push). (Houghton and Patel, 2015). While ISO 11064:4 concentrates more on the physical design of the workstations (for visibility, reach, comfort, and so on), it does not directly address issues of the content and design of the information itself. Also, it is a general framework that must be modified to the specific needs of a workstation. In practice, many maintenance workstations already exist (see Chapter 5) – the key issue is integrating new displays and workflows into that environment.

There is a more fundamental issue. ISO11064:4 aside, these frameworks take their starting point as data and data collection and then move through increasing levels of complexity to deliver prognostics and predictive intelligence. While this approach may make sense in terms of software and hardware architecture, it means that the intelligent support offered to the end-user is often shaped by the nature of data – this can sometimes mean the wrong data and often means too much data. As discussed in this book, this approach has to be complemented by an approach that puts operator decision-making at the heart of the process and derives requirements for data and information presentation.

One ISO that is firmly focused on user-centred design is ISO9241-210 Human-centred design for interactive systems. This general ISO introduces the main principles of user-centred design for an interactive product or service. We discuss this ISO and its relevance in greater depth in Chapter 4.

2.6 CHAPTER SUMMARY

This chapter has defined what we mean by remote condition monitoring and predictive maintenance – a systemic approach to combining sensor data, algorithms, and analysis to predict the state of assets. The application of predictive maintenance to various domains has been discussed, and we present one domain, rail, in-depth. The concern, however, is that this technology is data-driven, and there is little guidance on how to present meaningful guidance to operators. In the next chapter, we map out the human challenges of implementing predictive maintenance in greater depth.

3 Challenges of Remote Condition Monitoring

3.1 CHAPTER OVERVIEW

Chapter 2 detailed the technical nature of remote condition monitoring and highlighted some of the challenges with successful deployment. This chapter aims to give further details on the major human challenges of remote condition monitoring. This includes:

- Introducing the human challenges of remote condition monitoring
- Introducing the key principles of human factors of relevance to understand complex control environments
- Discussing the most important challenges in depth. These are:
  - Managing data volumes
  - Human–machine interface and alarm handling
  - Understanding automation
  - Centralised versus distributed control
  - Organisational challenges

3.2 CHALLENGES OF REMOTE CONDITION MONITORING

In the previous chapter, we introduced remote condition monitoring and the idea that it serves an important purpose in monitoring and maintaining the availability of assets and systems. We also introduced the idea that this is achieved through a multitude of different technologies working together to deliver information to an operator and discussed how this was relevant to an example context – the rail domain.

Despite the potential, the practice may not always deliver what is hoped for. Interviews with experts in predictive maintenance across multiple sectors as early as 1998 (Aktan et al. 1998) noted three main topics of health condition monitoring:

1. Knowledge required for diagnosing problems
2. Technology necessary for transmitting the knowledge
3. People who will work with the technology

Amongst these three topics, diagnosis and technology (items 1 and 2) have focused on significant research and practice. There have been many deployments in multiple sectors (some of the examples noted in Chapter 2 of this book). Topic 3 (i.e., people) is more difficult to tackle and has received less attention.

DOI: 10.1201/9781315587288-3

Negenborn et al. (2010) reviewed health condition monitoring in various domains and listed a number of challenges. These include:

1. Acquiring a deeper understating of their socio-technical interactions
2. Understanding the effects of automation on the overall system
3. Issues associated with system flexibility, reliability, safety, and quality of service
4. A need for a well-defined decision-making process within such multi-level, multi-actor, and dynamic systems

Again, these issues, particularly the first, second, and fourth, have only received limited attention. In interviews with experts from across a number of predictive maintenance implementations, Golightly et al. (2018) found that there are concerns that unless predictive maintenance technology can be designed in a way that meets the needs of operators, it often goes unused and fails to deliver the necessary benefits. Similarly, work in metro systems (Kefalidou et al., 2015; Ciocoiu et al., 2017) has highlighted the problems of integrating predictive maintenance technologies within pre-existing maintenance regimes.

There is also a wealth of anecdotal evidence, talking to operators who work with condition monitoring and prognostics systems. They can be difficult to use, are poorly integrated into the work environment, or have been subject to limited (or no) acceptance. Consequently, millions of pounds of investments may be wasted, and, more importantly, organisations have been discouraged from introducing innovation and change to the workplace.

This is not a specific problem that is unique to remote condition monitoring systems. The types of innovation we have described in this book so far have several features and characteristics common in the roll-out of the technology. The rest of the chapter describes these challenges in greater detail, as they form the basis for the human factors works in the rest of this book. Before discussing specific challenges, we introduce the general principles of human factors.

3.3   HUMAN FACTORS

Human Factors or Ergonomics (often used interchangeably) has been a significant scientific and practical field since the 1940s. There are many textbooks that give a thorough introduction to the field and its concepts, theories, and methods. In Chapters 3 and 4, we introduce some of the basic ideas of human factors and ergonomics. However, the interested reader could find out more from professional bodies such as the International Ergonomics Association (https://iea.cc/), Chartered Institute of Ergonomics and Human Factors (https://www.ergonomics.org.uk/), or the Human Factors and Ergonomics Society (https://www.hfes.org/). Introductory texts include Shorrock and Williams (2016) or Wickens et al. (2004) and the first chapter of Wilson and Sharples (2015), amongst many others.

For Wilson and Sharples (2015), human factors/ergonomics (HFE) refers to the "theory and practice of learning about human characteristics and capabilities, and then using that understanding to improve people's interaction with the things they use and within the environments in which they do so" (Wilson and Sharples, 2015). This definition suggests that both theory and practice should be in place, requiring an understanding of human needs, socio-demographic characteristics, and physical and cognitive abilities that lead to tangible design recommendations to design or improve a product or service. It is very much an applied discipline. Human factors specialists are not merely evaluators (although a big part of their role is to critique) – they, ultimately, influence or specify the design of systems, products, and/or services.

Physical HFE refers to the understanding of the physical aspects of action and interaction and the environmental context (e.g., temperature, illumination level, accessibility) to ensure that the design fits the environment and the design supports the user's physical characteristics. Physical aspects of HFE have been a major part of human performance reviews, occupational ergonomics, and the design of workplaces. It also covers anthropometrics. Much of physical ergonomics also relates to physical work – manual handling, upper limb injuries, working in extremes of cold or heat, and the physical design of equipment such as personal protective equipment (PPE).

Cognitive aspects of HFE refer to thinking, sensing, perceiving, responding, and decision-making elements of interaction. All interactions require some form of understanding of the context, information processing, and decision-making. Reviewing cognitive aspects requires understanding user perceptions, mental models, problem-solving, decision-making, and contributing factors such as expertise and learning. Despite decades of work in cognitive ergonomics and great breakthroughs in understanding and exploring complex control settings, there is still much to be done in this field, particularly now as we see complex settings where multiple people, technologies, products, and systems work together as part of a Joint Cognitive System (Hollnagel and Woods, 2005). Growing complexities due to recent technological advancements raised by artificial intelligence (AI) and machine learning (ML) have only increased the need for suitable, feasible, and effective ways of understanding how people and machines work together.

Organisational aspects of HFE are concerned with wider settings of interaction and broader aspects that influence socio-technical systems. Some of the elements that should be considered as part of organisational ergonomics include training, human performance, safety culture, change management, job satisfaction, and leadership. Also, it is essential to point out that work does not happen in a social vacuum, and the social and personal elements that people bring to their work are critical in our understanding of how to design effective technologies and systems.

Table 3.1 provides some examples of typical human factors issues that we could come across in the major areas of physical, cognitive, and organisational ergonomics in the context of railway maintenance and remote condition monitoring.

TABLE 3.1

Typical Topics in Ergonomics and Human Factors and Relevance to Remote Condition Monitoring

Area	Example topic	Relevance to remote condition monitoring
Physical	Manual handling	Trackwork involves the lifting and positioning of equipment, assets, and materials. Better planning through remote condition monitoring can reduce the need for redundant work and therefore reduce manual handling exposure (Riley, 2006).
	Environmental conditions	Inspection and maintenance often have to take place at night or in cold, wet, or enclosed conditions (e.g., working in a tunnel). These conditions can impair human performance and present hazards. Asset management can reduce the need for this work through remote sensing of the asset state (Golightly et al., 2013b).
	Display screen equipment (DSE)	Remote condition monitoring workstations must be designed to comply with the needs of good DSE design (e.g., http://www.hse.gov.uk/msd/dse/) and to ensure that issues with glare, size, and portability are not deterring from the effectiveness of remote condition monitoring.
Cognitive	Situation awareness	Situation awareness supports maintaining an accurate mental model of the present status of a system while being able to predict its future state (Endsley, 1995). While remote condition monitoring can support this wide overview of many assets and their current and future state, automation should also be designed to keep the user "in the loop".
	Human–computer interaction	Asset management and remote condition monitoring should be designed to optimise information presentation and apply principles of user-centred design (Houghton and Patel, 2015). This is critical when addressing the area of data visualisation.
	Expertise and decision-making	Expertise in remote condition monitoring comprises knowledge about assets, their likely behaviour, and coping strategies. These strategies influence decision-making. Future design should support and complement the most adaptive strategies (Dadashi et al., 2021).
Organisational	Team coordination	Asset management and maintenance involve the coordination between multiple roles, particularly where an unexpected failure stops the service. Processes and technologies should be designed to reflect team coordination.

(Continued)

TABLE 3.1   (CONTINUED)

Typical Topics in Ergonomics and Human Factors and Relevance to Remote Condition Monitoring

Area	Example topic	Relevance to remote condition monitoring
	Safety culture	Safety culture is the perception of individuals and organisations to maintain and develop safe working practices. Maintenance processes can be improved and monitored to ensure all parties (including asset management staff) know what is required for a positive, safe working environment (Farrington-Darby et al., 2005 and Guldenmund, 2000).
	Leadership and change management	In response to change, the management and up-skilling of staff and safety culture must be driven from the top of the organisation (Ciociou et al., 2015; Golightly et al., 2018). Leadership is vital to minimise training times, maximise the adaptation of working practices, and encourage worker buy-in.

We can view physical, cognitive, and organisational factors as being closely interlinked. While studies or problems tend to focus on one aspect over another, it is often the case that other factors come into play. For example, we could look at a very physical activity such as lifting heavy materials (e.g., concrete troughing) in a work environment (e.g., laying new signalling and telecommunications cables at the trackside). This is a physical task, and the hazards are primarily physical (back injury through lifting heavy weights, dropping troughs on feet, trapping hands, etc.). But there is still a cognitive element (have the staff been trained and know good manual handling techniques? Do they know how to use manual handling aids that might lower risk? Do they understand where they are lifting from and to minimise time lifting?). Furthermore, there is the organisational element (Are there enough people on track so that two- and three-person lifts are possible? Has the work been planned with enough time so that people can plan their lifts, or do they feel they have to rush? Do they know each other well enough to ask for help, or is there a "macho" culture where helping each other is a sign of weakness?).

While most of what we discuss in this book concerns cognitive and, to some extent, organisational factors, maintenance, and similar control rooms still feature the interconnectivity of physical, cognitive, and organisational. Can I hear alarms? Can I see them? These are physical factors, but they influence my ability to make decisions and process information. Also, has the organisation thought about how to procure a coherent set of technologies and integrate them to support a change in working culture and support user adoption?

Wilson and Sharples (2015) structure the aim of HFE as depicted in Figure 3.1, and people and organisational aims are both listed. The diagram emphasises the importance and the need for a macro-level understanding of the workplace, and it allows for enhancements in design, supports performance, and influences work culture.

One of the fundamental pillars of the human factors approach is that it is a systems discipline. People are considered together with technology (often including automation) and as part of organisations and processes. All of these factors must be considered together to fully understand how to develop performance, maintain safety, and prevent accidents (Wilson and Sharples, 2015).

Typically, we call these systems socio-technical – where people and technology work together in a complex environment towards a common goal (Rankin et al., 2014). Note the use of the word "complex". This is more than just "complicated" (there are many parts). Complex is used more specifically to mean systems where (1) there is high dimensionality – there are multiple goals or criteria for performance (e.g., time, quality, safety). These may be competing, so a key aspect of overall system performance is managing these goals. Also, there may be no specific endpoint to a goal. However, instead, performance is a process of continuously balancing parameters both within a function. Across the system as a whole (2), there is interdependence – in complex systems, the performance and success of any function are closely linked to the performance of one or more functions. This can lead to non-linearity. The results of one function do not neatly feed into another but instead are constantly feeding back into each other (Flach, 2012).

Railways, nuclear power, manufacturing, process control, and space operations are examples of complex socio-technical systems (e.g., see Wilson, 2014). They are also all systems that can include remote condition monitoring, and therefore the deployment of new technology needs to take a systems view. Hence, methods have been developed such as cognitive work analysis (CWA) (see Chapter 4) that try and describe the whole of the system – its functioning, the constraints, pressure on the work, and the stages involved – so we can understand the role of people within these systems.

While much of the initial motivation behind human factors was driven by "human error" (though even that term is debated [Reason, 1990; Dekker, 2004]), there has been a move away from acting as disaster preventing, accident investigating researchers to seeking out how people perform in a way that maintains, and preserves safety (Hollnagel et al., 2015). The emphasis of HFE is also just as much on wellbeing and performance at work, and the techniques of human factors have increasingly informed areas such as user-centred experiences and product design (e.g., Mack and Sharples, 2009). As a result of active participation in the design and deployment of technical and socio-technical systems, human factors work has become an integral part of the design to improve the user interface interaction (ISO 9241-210) (discussed further in Chapter 4). To do that, we need to understand the context and sequence of the use of technologies and processes in a multi-disciplinary and applied way. As a result, human factors draws from the theory and practice of neighbouring disciplines such as human–computer interaction, psychology, physiology, sociology, and anthropology.

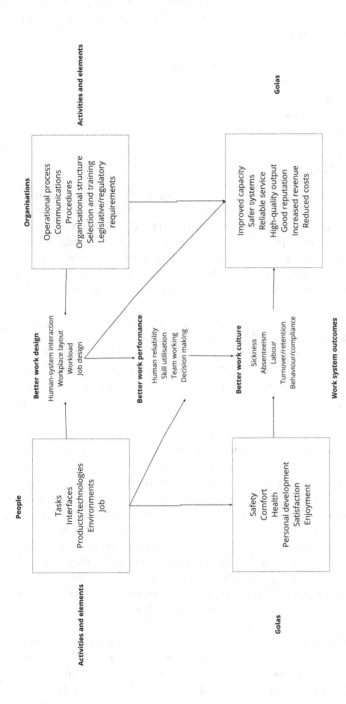

FIGURE 3.1 Aims of ergonomics/human factors taken from Wilson and Sharples (2015). E/HF can be seen in the context of its objectives which are the wellbeing of the people and organisations

We will cover the methods of human factors further in Chapter 4. For now, we dive down into some of the specific challenges of remote condition monitoring. Particularly common and crucial challenges are:

- Managing data (e.g., volume, integrity, reliability)
- Human–machine interface and alarm handling
- Understanding automation
- Centralised versus distributed control
- Organisational change

3.4   MANAGING DATA

Initially, systems to monitor assets were beset by a fundamental bottleneck. Limited sensor systems and transfer mechanisms meant that only limited amounts of information could be gathered from low-resolution sensors via comparatively slow data transfer mechanisms (for example, via telephone modems with data rates at best falling in the low hundreds of kilobits a second). At that stage, data collection and storage were the key technical challenges to be addressed. The derivation of useful information from the data was largely limited to raising alerts and alarms as monitored processes moved out of expected tolerances.

As sensor and communication technologies have matured, however, and the cost of data storage has dropped, they are being used in more places and are able to collect (and send) ever greater quantities of data. For example, the Network Rail New Measurement Train (see Figure 3.2) – a diesel train set customised with on-board track monitoring equipment – can generate terabytes of data within a matter of hours for distances of track that would have previously taken weeks for staff to inspect by walking the track.

Therefore, one of the most important challenges facing asset management and remote condition monitoring systems is managing the volume of data generated by the system. This data needs to be processed and presented in a manner that makes sense to the intended user, but it is impossible to scroll through or search at such volumes. Also, when a track worker visibly inspects a track to see cracks or defects, this "data" immediately has meaning. Raw streams of data on track geometry, etc. do not necessarily have this instantaneous meaning to anyone but the most skilled maintenance technician. Therefore, some level of technical analysis is required first.

In addition, one of the recurring questions in designing dynamic control environments is whether providing more information leads to better operational decisions. The idea that every piece of information should be made available is increasingly tempting (and in safety-critical domains often mandatory) but has become a potential obstacle for designers and operators.

In order to ensure the effective implementation of a remote condition monitoring system, data obtained from the infrastructure must be transformed (i.e., collected, configured, and calibrated) into useful information, as well as being exploited in the most optimal way (Crainic, 2009). Moreover, the operator should know the effect of the measured condition on the overall operation of the asset in order to predict

FIGURE 3.2 An image of a new measurement train. Credit: Network Rail

potential failures and behaviours of the asset in the future (Houghton and Patel, 2015).

Failing to define the correct purpose for the data may result in the system presenting too little information or overloading the operator with inappropriate information. Hence it is important to realise what level of detail is required. For instance, in railway asset management and remote condition monitoring systems, does the operator require a simple binary (working/failed) assessment of the status of an asset or a more detailed measurement? In addition, it is interesting to consider how a static metric compares with baselines, trends over time, comparison with other assets, or interactions with other system properties. For example, data about the volume of water in a drain becomes much more useful when combined with surface water levels, drainage flow rates, and accurate, localised, and real-time weather forecasting. The next step is to use machine learning to predict where flooding is likely – providing advanced insight and the drill-down data as required. Also, all adaptation and calibration of new forms of data and sensing must be appropriately resourced by people with the requisite knowledge.

3.5 HUMAN–MACHINE INTERACTION, INCLUDING ALARM HANDLING

Because the maintenance operator is remote from the asset, information is communicated to the operator not through their sense *on site*, but through a human–machine interface (HMI). The HMI is therefore critical to how the operator interprets the state of the world and makes their decisions. Typically, this is presented on a screen or on a number of screens at a workstation.

Technically, the HMI might be delivered through standalone software, or through browser-based information. The latter is often preferred as it means that the software demand at the operator (or "client") end is relatively light (or "thin") and thus modifications and updates to processing and software can all occur centrally. The downside is that the HMI is therefore constrained by the functional capabilities of the web browser. Also, information may be presented on handheld devices such as phones or tablets. Again, while this might increase the utility of the HMI in making it available anywhere (e.g., for maintenance staff out of track [Dadashi et al., 2010]), this can put constraints on the visibility of the information. Furthermore, operators handling multiple assets may be faced with five different vendors and five different apps with no integration or consistency between the information.

Dense information presentation, the use of codes or unclear iconography, and the limited use of colour can all impede the user. Also, HMI refers not only to how information is presented but how a user interacts with information and functions. This might be the logic (or lack of it) in interaction sequences and the steps required to complete a task, the lack of feedback or unclear error messages, or simple (but critical) issues such as prompting users before they make a change which they cannot undo (Nielsen, 2020). Operators often have a sequential, rule-based approach towards accessing and interpreting sources of information. Presenting this information in a cohesive way that matches operators' mental models and cognitive processing is essential for designing effective decision aids.

Some of these issues (i.e., information presentation, visibility of system status, consistency and understanding of mental models) can prevent a user from working with an application altogether. Others may, on their own, be minor inconveniences but multiplied up over 10s or even 100s of interactions in a day, which becomes a substantial source of frustration and ultimately rejection. Human factors-based digital skills such as information architecture, information design, interaction design, and graphical design are critical to success.

There are also considerations about how a user might access and navigate large amounts of information. The principal mechanism might be one of "pushing" or prompting the user through alarms. Alarms range from simple prompts for an operator to carry out further actions, including making diagnoses, through to semantically rich messages carrying verbal, textual, or pictorial information about the source or cause of the abnormality. With the shift to prognostic systems, alarms will move from informing the operator of a current or recent event (e.g., failure of a piece of infrastructure) to include anticipatory alarms that warn the operator of an emerging risk (e.g., potential failure or degradation of asset performance). The use of this kind of pre-emptive alarm is likely to be highly relevant to predictive asset management and health monitoring system in future railways.

Successful implementation of alarm display systems, however, is not straightforward.

Poor alarm handling has been a contributory factor in a number of safety-critical incidents such as Three Mile Island in 1979 (Campbell, 1988) and the Texaco refinery explosion in 1994 (Wilkinson and Lucas, 2002; Timms, 2009). In transportation, aircraft hazard reports confirm that alarm problems contributed to about 50% of all of the incidents that were recorded between the years 1984 and 1994 (Gilson et al., 2001). Other examples include the Ladbroke Grove train accident (Cullen, 2000; though see Stanton and Baber, 2006, for a different perspective), and the Channel Tunnel Fire (Brown, 1999), and effective alarm handling continues to be a major safety issue (Wilkinson and Lucas, 2002).

However, alarms are not the only means of accessing information in the human–machine interface. First, a user may need to navigate information in order to interpret alarms (i.e., to perform diagnoses). Also, there are situations in more strategic or planning roles where a user may actively wish to search or browse across information – for example, to see whether a suite of assets is operating less efficiently than usual and may be ready for repair. In both cases, the user needs an HMI that allows structured searching of data. This means that the navigation or "information architecture" of data and information must be amenable to the activities and needs of maintenance staff (Houghton and Patel, 2015). However, this is often an afterthought in design, making maintenance systems slow and cumbersome to use.

3.6 UNDERSTANDING AUTOMATION

Predictive technology such as asset management is dependent on some degree of automation and decision support for an operator. This automation is in part due to the analytical overhead of sensing multiple data streams from multiple assets and in part due to the algorithms for calculating the prediction of risk and failure associated with an asset. The volume of sensed data and the complexity of calculation necessitate automation.

Automating various functions to improve and enhance railway operations has become increasingly prevalent. This is due to growing demands on railway capacity and parallel pressures on costs of operation (McNulty, 2011). Despite their obvious appeal, automated control processes in the railway and in other sectors have not always had the expected outcomes.

When automation moves from purely physical tasks to aspects of cognitive control (planning, rescheduling, decision-making) (Mayer et al., 2009), a number of issues can occur. These include a reduced sense of engagement and involvement for operational staff, who find difficulty in re-establishing control if the automation hands back some or all processes (Balfe et al., 2012; Sebok and Wickens, 2017), also known as "out-of-loop". Also, while automation can draw on huge amounts of data to make decisions, it often lacks the heuristic knowledge and awareness of secondary cues that are vital for effective planning and prioritisation (Ouelhadj and Petrovic, 2009; Ramchurn et al., 2016).

While automation can in theory ease the workload of the operator, there is often a need for the operator to perceive and interpret information regarding the status and actions of the automation itself (Balfe et al., 2012). This, too, becomes a further stream of information to be assessed and factored into decision-making. Unfortunately, in the least successful cases, design for human-automation integration goes no further than building a human–machine interface that generates data about the automated process (Oborski, 2004; Wu et al., 2016). These data are often raw, incomplete, or both, and require prohibitive overheads on the part of the operator to interpret in a timely, accurate manner. Other attempts to integrate automation have taken a functional allocation approach. One or more functional aspects of a process are identified as amenable to automation, and this aspect of the process is taken out of the control of the human and placed in the hands of an automated system. While this approach appears pragmatic, it can have significant negative repercussions for awareness of other tasks that remain within the remit of the human operator, for the maintenance of human skill, knowledge, and motivation, and for the ability of humans to re-establish effective control if the automation fails (Bainbridge, 1983; Fuld, 1993; Mayer et al., 2011), which, over time, can also lead to a longer-term loss of understanding about how a system works.

In the case of maintenance and monitoring systems, if the reasoning behind decisions is not clear, then users either become inappropriately over-reliant, or lack trust in, outputs and decisions. Also, with real-time automation systems, the need to keep on top of what the automation is doing, particularly when the HMI for the automation is difficult to understand, becomes its own source of workload (Sharples et al., 2011).

3.7 CENTRALISED VERSUS DISTRIBUTED CONTROL

The ability to access the status of information about assets at a distance of sometimes hundreds (or even thousands) of miles means control environments are moving more towards integration and centralisation. While this has many advantages, it requires new ways of thinking about how work will be coordinated and the implications of putting several functions in close proximity.

One way of understanding advanced remote condition monitoring and its potential obstacles is to view it as a supervisory control problem. Sheridan and Hennessy (1984, pp. 8) defined supervisory control as: "activities of the human supervisor who interacts via a computer with a complex and semiautonomous process". Machines transfer sensed and modified information of an on-going physical process to a human operator. In other words, the technical system acts as a mediator between the environment and the operator (Sheridan, 1997).

Sheridan and Sheridan (2002) also defined the term supervisory control as analogous to the normal supervisor and the relationship between supervisor and subordinates. The more intelligent and competent the subordinates are, the less supervisors will have to intervene. It is now common in supervisory control environments for these subordinates to be replaced with computer systems (Sheridan, 2002). This will be the case with many automated asset management technologies.

SUPERVISORY CONTROL BEHAVIOUR

Supervisory control behaviour consists of five basic elements: plan, teach, monitor, intervene, and learn. These elements are briefly explained below.

Plan: the human operator has to understand how the process works and what the system objectives and constraints are, enabling them to decide on a control strategy (e.g., decide on alarm priorities).

Teach: to instruct the computer, based on the planned programme (e.g., define alarm priorities in colour coding or setting a threshold level on the machine).

Monitor: systems taught or instructed as in the previous stage will work automatically; the human operator needs to ensure that the system and these automated features are working properly. The problem arises when there are too many variables to monitor, which is almost always the case in today's complex socio-technical environments. A potential solution to assist operators in monitoring is notifying them of any abnormalities through alarms (as will be discussed in Chapter 6).

Intervene: the operator needs to intervene when they find anomalies or if any abnormalities are observed. Problems arise when the operators are uncertain as to whether they should intervene, due to the lack of information or lack of transparency between the human operator and the automated component. Furthermore, when operators are faced with a high workload or stress, they might fail to detect the need for intervention (Sheridan, 2002).

Learn: operators learn from their experience and apply their knowledge in future supervisory control situations, events, and roles.

Interaction with user interfaces of a remote condition monitoring system could resemble those noted for a supervisory control system. However, the option for automating aspects (and creating an asset management system) would mean that the nature of these activities, their function allocation, and hence information requirements might change.

On the other hand, with the introduction of centralised and integrated control systems, different members of staff with different roles are responsible together for broader and more complex problem-solving situations (i.e., multi-agent control shared between signalling, disruption management, and track-worker protection functions [Golightly et al., 2013a]). There is therefore a paradox in that maintenance is increasingly centralised but is also more distributed.

Introducing new technology that aims to centralise and integrate existing technologies will affect the way people perceive and perform their roles. This is particularly because new methods of diagnosis and prognosis will be adopted, meaning that experienced operators will have to depart from their traditional ways of working.

The challenge of implementing automation in the form of asset management for the railway is a particularly acute example, because of the multiple dimensions over which the system can be considered "distributed" and the complexities that result in terms of both building a reliable architecture and a human-interpretable output. First, the assets themselves are distributed. There may be millions of assets in a technical system as broad as a national railway infrastructure, with many sensors required to present an accurate picture of an asset as complex as a bridge or level crossing. Synthesising and presenting such complex data to support effective action requires a detailed understanding of the context in which asset management work takes place.

Second, the analysis of the data (the "intelligence") may be distributed between analysis localised in the sensors themselves, further analysis at some central point, and analysis conducted by an operator in order to diagnose and act upon an alarm. Therefore, a clear understanding is needed of the process of transfer between pure data into knowledge for action, and where the functions that support that transfer should lie.

Finally, in the socio-technical system that is the railway, people are themselves distributed both physically and across roles, and their decisions are distributed over time. A local maintenance engineer may need only critical diagnostic information in order to effect emergency repairs on an asset that is about to fail; a strategic planner in a central office may be using analysis based on weeks, months, or years of data to prioritise renewal regimes.

3.8   ORGANISATIONAL CHALLENGE

One of the fundamental pillars of an intelligent predictive approach is a shift in emphasis from scheduled and reactive work to more pro-active work (from "find and fix" to "predict and prevent"). The technical and human considerations outlined so far ultimately have organisational implications and require a fundamental re-ordering and re-structuring of work. This has implications around organisational approaches to factors such as skills and training. In addition, it will impact the number of staff required, their location of work, their competencies, and their work organisation.

Predictive maintenance moves activity from a regular event, often conducted out-of-hours and therefore often at a better rate of pay for unsociable hours to something that is more desk-based, more 9 to 5, and involves less fieldwork (an aspect of the work that was often quite appealing for engineers who like to be "hands on" with equipment). The other side of that knowledge coin is that people will require new technical skills. Having a body of existing IT competence is deemed a critical factor in successful e-maintenance deployment (Aboelmaged, 2014). This requires appropriate competency for the staff working the system in terms of both technical skills and IT management skills (Chowdhury and Akram, 2013).

Also, different technologies may be procured at different times from different suppliers. This leads to a risk of siloes developing between different functional units within an organisation based on which specific technology they are working with, with limited knowledge exchange (Koochaki and Bouwhuis, 2008). This can be exacerbated by a lack of a common frame of reference (Koochaki and Bouwhuis, 2008) for what remote condition monitoring or predictive maintenance means for different functions. Ultimately, the deployment of predictive maintenance technology needs a significant culture change in the organisation to one that proactively and coherently embraces predictive maintenance in terms of its resourcing, planning, and procurement. As with all forms of culture change, this requires appropriate leadership (Armstrong and Sambamurthy, 1999).

Finally, these changes are shaping the relationships between organisations. Previously, an organisation would operate, maintain, and sometimes even build its own assets. This is changing to a model where the builder of an asset may monitor the product on behalf of the asset owner/operator (Smith, 2013) or could be third parties who take on responsibility for product and customer support (Kajko-Mattsson et al., 2010), but understanding client needs can be a complex process. Also, both the service provider and service user should acknowledge the need for a higher level of collaboration and human contact in comparison to traditional product sales contracts. There are also concerns around trust and of different stakeholders having access to performance data (Golightly et al., 2013a). When predictive maintenance can be deployed effectively, however, there may be multiple gains to be enjoyed as additional, unexpected uses and benefits are found for different stakeholders across the supply chain (Chowdhury and Akram,2013; Golightly et al., 2018) (see Table 3.2).

TABLE 3.2
Highlights of the Challenges of Remote Condition Monitoring

Theme	Summary
Human–machine interface and alarm handling	The need to explore digital touchpoints, devices, information capturing, and presentation. The key challenge is to understand the context of work in order to develop optimal information presentation strategies (right time, right place, and right information).
Understanding automation	Creating an in-depth understanding of aspects of automation, different levels of automation, and their importance to the activities conducted by operators and their association with existing workload, situational awareness, and reliability of work.
Centralised versus distributed	To understand the benefits and barriers of both centralised and distributed models of supervisory control. Understanding technical and operational considerations and facilitating planning, up-skilling, and retraining in preparation for transitions from centralised to distributed or vice versa.
Organisational change	Exploring the important aspects of user acceptance and engagement when being introduced to innovative solutions. Creating a road map to facilitate an on-going conversation with existing and prospective workforce to ensure the organisational changes are primed for future systems and work settings.

3.9 CHAPTER SUMMARY

This chapter highlights the challenges of remote condition monitoring, which we summarise in Table 3.2. This list is not exhaustive, but these are the challenges we believe to be most critical and most often overlooked when designing technologies that need to consider the user in a remote condition monitoring context. One of the primary aims of the work in this book is to explore and confirm these challenges in greater depth. This is covered in Chapters 5–8. Before going into these studies in the next chapter, we introduce the basic principles of human factors methods to understand user needs for complex socio-technical systems such as railway asset management and remote condition monitoring.

4 Human Factors to Explore Remote Condition Monitoring

4.1 CHAPTER OVERVIEW

Chapter 2 introduced remote condition monitoring, and Chapter 3 focused on human factors and the human challenges of remote condition monitoring. This chapter introduces important methods to understand the context of work when using remote condition monitoring. This can help with the design of both current technology and future advances such as predictive maintenance. There are also representative of the studies described in the second part of the book. It is important to note that this chapter is not aiming to provide a comprehensive description of techniques but instead provides a high-level and practical overview of the research studies presented in the second part of this book. A much more extensive review of key techniques is available in Wilson and Sharples (2015) and Stanton et al. (2013) amongst many others. The key objectives of this chapter are therefore:

1. To introduce the importance of the methods, and the relation between contextual and sequential methods, and the role of the user-centred design process
2. To present data collection methods used to understand remote condition monitoring needs
3. To present data analysis and representation methods to describe asset management

4.2 USER-CENTRED DESIGN AND ISO 9241-210

The fundamental philosophy of this book is one of user-centred design. Rather than innovation being led by technology, new capabilities or new technical/engineering challenges, user-centred design considers, upfront, the needs and abilities of users. It provides a complete framework from project inception through to delivery and beyond to ensure that any system fits with what users want, within their context of use. It has been extensively used in all manner of projects, from nuclear control room design, to autonomous vehicle HMI, and through to common consumer products such as smartphone services.

The user-centred design approach is described in human-centred design activities (ISO 9241-210, 2010). There are a number of points to note about this process. First,

DOI: 10.1201/9781315587288-4

it is a multi-stage process starting at project inception. Too often, if a usability or ergonomic analysis takes place, it occurs right at the end of a project at some kind of trials phase, or even once the product or service has been deployed. The result is that changes are costly and technically difficult to make or may even be impossible, given the way the technology has been built. The user-centred design process positions the process up front, in the heart of development. This will require coordination with the development team and project managers.

Second, it is iterative and incremental. It anticipates that cycles of revision may be needed to get the design right and therefore multiple stages of user involvement and, in particular, evaluation, may be required using different techniques. The ISO can be incorporated into traditional "waterfall" processes as well as agile development.

Finally, it emphasises context. This means understanding not just how an ideal user might use the product but also understanding all the different tasks, motivations, and challenges that a user might face. Importantly. This means not just thinking about the software under development in isolation but also the relation with other software the user might need when performing their tasks. The major theme of this book is to understand the context of work relevant to remote condition monitoring, in order to inform and facilitate a user-centred design process.

4.3   UNDERSTANDING COMPLEX CONTROL CONTEXTS

The first step to conduct in any project is to understand the context of use. We often approach this in quite an organic way – to do a walk down, a site visit, or just a quick conversation with the client about their work. Ideally, this should be followed by a series of more focused interviews or experimental studies. However, it is necessary to embed human factors in a way that is a pragmatic use of resources (both for the human factors specialist and the project as a whole). It is simply not practical on all but very few projects to take an anthropological or ethnographic approach, where the researcher is immersed in the domain without interruption, nor are laboratory studies measuring variables sufficient to understand the complexity of a domain (Hoffman and Woods, 2000). It can also be difficult to mark the boundaries between qualitative and quantitative methods. Therefore, it is recommended to use a combination of methods to explore the context, systems, and human operators (Bainbridge, 1997). Methods need to be practical and make good use of resources.

One way of guiding the understanding of complex work settings and introducing a way to decompose this complexity is by focusing on sequential and contextual approaches. Sequential approaches focus on the sequence of the tasks and their relative cognition. It is very much rooted in system engineering with the aim to develop an almost algorithmic understanding of the world and consequently guide the design of closed control environments (e.g., power plants, chemical processing plants). More than just a simple task analysis, a sequential approach should also model the cognitive process as a sequence of activities. Rasmussen's decision ladder (1985) is one such example and one that we use later in the book.

Although sequential models provide a clear view of the stages of the activities required by the overall system, they do not state anything about the domain-specific factors that might shape work, or how it is performed. Therefore, it is important to develop a contextual understanding. The contextual approach attempts to explore the system from the limitations imposed on human operators through the environment (Rasmussen, 1985) as well as the wider context of use. In other words, this approach attempts to analyse cognition within its ambience. In the contextual approach, human behaviour is context-dependent, varying from one domain to another (Bainbridge, 1983).

Therefore, in order to develop an understanding of human behaviours and their cognition in complex control environments, contextual understanding is vital. "Contextual approach focuses on the overview, the temporary structure of inference built up in working storage to describe the task situation and how this provides the context for later processing and for the effective organisation of behaviour" (Bainbridge, 1997, pp. 352).

Also, since cognition is no longer bound to an individual human operator, understanding the information processing in these complex and multi-agent environments needs to include more than the tasks and artefacts utilised by one individual. Hutchins (1995) argues that early cognitive studies attempted to understand the human individual, leaving issues such as context, culture, and even history for later. This would not lead to a correct understanding of the domain, since those marginalised issues (context, culture, etc.) are at the core of human cognition. Understanding the social arrangements of work, how different roles interact, and the overall organisation is therefore vital for a full understanding of work. This can be done in a narrative way, through the use of scenarios (Rosson and Carrol, 2009), but can also be represented as more structured models. Abstraction hierarchy (Rasmussen, 1986; Bisantz and Vicente, 1994; Vicente, 1999) is one example of a structured contextual approach. More recently the emphasis has been on understanding "work as done" as opposed to "work as imagined" (Hollangel, 2017).

The key point to remember is that we don't need complicated or technologically sophisticated data collection and analysis techniques to facilitate sequential and contextual understanding of our work domain. We do need a good understanding of key methods and what we can/should expect from them. In the next section, we introduce some of these methods, and then later chapters describe these methods and demonstrate their applications in detail.

4.4 METHODS TO UNDERSTAND COMPLEX CONTROL ENVIRONMENTS

The section above has highlighted the need to go beyond sequential models, to also include the importance of context. This applies generally, and specifically when understanding decision-making, problem-solving, and information use. In the pursuit of understanding complex work settings, therefore, a broad range of methods of data collection and data analysis should be used (Hoffman and Woods, 2000). These can be split into two categories – those that allow us to capture data about the complex domain (data collection methods) and those that allow us to structure our understanding of the domain (data modelling methods). Table 4.1 presents an

TABLE 4.1
Overview of Methods Demonstrated in This Book

Purpose	Method/Approach	Description	Relevance to remote condition monitoring as applied in this book
Data collection	Semi-structure interview study	Interview studies provide an opportunity to collect data from different stakeholders. Semi-structured interviews suggest high-level questions to be discussed during the interview, and these will guide the flow of conversation while keeping the key focus open to each of the informants.	Chapter 5 presents an interview study with senior managers within the railway to define railway remote condition monitoring.
	Observations/field study	To explore the work environment, to study its capacities and limitations, and to understand the information resources available to users. These exploratory visits allow for a high-level understanding of the context of work and guide future in-depth studies.	All of the studies reported in Chapters 6 and 7 start with familiarisation and exploratory studies. These include viewing control rooms (electrical control and maintenance control) to become familiar with different functions, available technologies, and operators' roles and responsibilities.
	Critical decision method (Klein et al. 1989)	CDM is a knowledge elicitation technique used to capture users' cognitive processing. Participants are asked to think about a number of previous incidents and to describe their problem-solving and decision-making processes. This is facilitated through a number of probing questions (i.e., what was your cue, how did you deal with uncertainty, etc.).	Chapter 6 reports a CDM study of maintenance control room operators.
	Activity analysis	To guide observations of people's work, structured data collection can be used. This allows systematic data collection which can then be used to generate timeline analysis or to understand time on task.	Chapters 7 and 8 present a detailed data collection to develop an understanding of alarm handling in railway electrical control rooms.
	Cognitive task analysis	To provide a detailed understanding of system functions, tasks, and their corresponding cognitive activities. It allows an in-depth review of the complex socio-technical system.	Chapter 6 conducts a cognitive task analysis to review fault finding within railway maintenance control.

(Continued)

TABLE 4.1   (CONTINUED)
Overview of Methods Demonstrated in This Book

Purpose	Method/Approach	Description	Relevance to remote condition monitoring as applied in this book
Data modelling	Thematic content analysis	Qualitative data captured during interview studies will need to be analysed thematically. High-level concepts and research questions will guide the selection of relevant themes.	Chapter 5 presents the interview studies and thematic content analysis. Each interview has been coded from three sets of themes: (1) human factors issues, (2) general definition of remote condition monitoring, and (3) information processing associated with asset management.
	Scenarios	Textual description of an event that describes various features as a narrative.	Chapter 5 describes the outputs of remote condition monitoring.
	Decision ladders	Provides a template to document sequences of decision-making activities and their associated cognitive processing and highlights potential shortcuts taken by users.	Chapter 6 presents decision ladders of fault finding within railway maintenance control.
	Cognitive work analysis	A programme of research to develop a fundamental understanding of a work domain and its cognitive processes.	Chapters 7 and 8 present data collection and analysis conducted to inform cognitive work analysis of alarm handling in railway electrical control rooms.

overview of the methods used in this book. The rest of this chapter briefly introduces these methods.

4.5   DATA COLLECTION

4.5.1   SEMI-STRUCTURED INTERVIEW

Interview studies are simply talking to users about their experience with the system, service, or product. It can be quite informal (just a quick phone call or chat) or very structured with a fixed set of questions. A semi-structured interview is a very common and effective form of an interview study as it allows for following an agenda while providing participants/interviewees with the flexibility to discuss what interests them. The semi-structured interview is a method that enables capturing qualitative data and guides the investigator towards an understanding and exploring various aspects of the complex work setting (Robson and McCartan, 2016).

They are different from unstructured interviews, in the sense that they have a number of pre-defined questions to guide the study. However, since the domain is not fully known, the structure of the questions addressed in this study can only be partially designed. Prior to forming this structure, the researcher has to become familiar with the domain, to ensure that the questions asked in the interview are targeting the research objectives. The more structure we add to an interview study, the less flexible the data collection will be (which might not be something we want especially if we want to uncover and discuss innovative solutions, or the use of tacit knowledge when working). The least structured are appropriate to ideate and think of disruptive designs, but they are very difficult to structure and analyse afterwards. Hence, the semi-structured interview provides a good balance of collecting relevant information, providing flexibility to capture the unknowns and also some structure to aid with data analysis and synthesis.

Throughout this book, we have used semi-structured interview studies to inform the concept of remote condition monitoring and asset management (ultimately Intelligent Infrastructure). Details of data collection, analysis, and synthesis are noted in Chapter 5 and again in Chapter 8.

4.5.2   OBSERVATIONAL STUDY

Often the first step towards exploring a complex system, observational studies are at the core of understanding any socio-technical environment. There are different types of observational studies including the direct, indirect, and participatory observation that can be used to inform and guide different aspects of a project. Familiarisation observations assist the investigator in obtaining an understanding of the study's domain. Field studies investigate certain functions within that domain (e.g., alarm handling in a railway electrical control room). Field studies are useful for understanding the domain in a more comprehensive way (Bisantz and Drury, 2005), and to enable the investigators to identify significant issues in complex socio-technical settings. They require detailed planning before they can be effective, and a lack of planning is probably the most common mistake when trying to use this technique. Researchers who just dive into the domain without prior review of that environment consequently waste or underuse this valuable resource. Finally, they need the consent and agreement of those being observed. At first, this can be difficult, and the aims of the study need to be clearly communicated both in written form and verbally. However, with care, and an open mind, observed participants will often engage with the process, opening up about their work and a multitude of factors that shape their performance and their thoughts about potential future options (Golightly and Young, 2022).

While observations can be performed in an informal way, there are means to make data collection more structured. Sundstrom and Salvador (1995) have noted that conducting structured field studies can interconnect with exploratory observational studies, in order to develop an understanding of user needs. Structured studies are time consuming to set up and even more challenging to analyse, but they provide a lens to explore work in its natural setting. The core reason for using a more structured data collection approach in human factors studies is to support two things: (1) to facilitate the quantification of an improvement in the human–machine interaction and (2) to perform a structured comparison between a set of pre-defined design recommendations (Rolo and Diaz-Cabrera, 2005).

One example of designing and collecting data in a more structured way is to record. Recording video data is a useful tool, which enables the researcher to review and analyse the activities during the field studies with more accuracy (Robson and McCartan, 2016). This method is of specific interest to explore socio-technical environments since it facilitates capturing a number of sources of information, such as the operators' interactions with the technical system, and their conversations with other team members. However, it can be quite daunting to analyse and require special skill sets to utilise the vast range of data to inform appropriate design decisions.

In addition, human behaviours, while interacting with cognitive systems, are not usually in the form of observable actions. One way to deal with this challenge is a verbal protocol (walkthrough/talk through). Simply put, users are asked to talk about their experience and walk us through the actions while conducting the activity and in doing so describe their thinking process, challenges, frustrations, and wonders. Verbal protocol analysis enables capturing these mental processes either by having the operator explain their actions while performing the tasks or by following the completion of the activity (Bainbridge and Sanderson, 2005).

Various forms of observations were conducted in the research studies presented in this book to inform the alarm handling and fault finding in rail electrical control rooms and maintenance control rooms (Chapters 6 and 7).

4.5.3 Cognitive Task Analysis (CTA)

Task analysis forms an envelope of procedures and contextual facts, which can elaborate human behaviour in working environments (Sheperd and Stammers, 2005).

The change in the role of human operators, from actors to thinkers, led to the developing of framework which can capture both physical activities as well as mental processes in complex control settings.

CTA aims to cover three aspects of human–machine interaction: contents of technical skill, context, and mental models (Cacciabue, 1998). Therefore, it can provide researchers with information regarding the working environment, structures of cognitive plans, and links between tasks and goals. To achieve this level of understanding of tasks, different forms of data collection and analysis are employed. These methods have to be more focused on internal processes and mental operations than merely observing physical interactions. Various techniques have been adopted to enable this level of detail.

O'Hare et al. (1998) confirm that CTA is an appropriate approach to exploring complex cognitive tasks. However, the effectiveness of the approach is highly dependent on the researcher's knowledge of the domain, as well as the extent and quality of resources available to the study.

4.5.4 CRITICAL DECISION METHOD

Towards understanding and appreciating the complex socio-technical system, a very common and simple method is the critical decision method (CDM). CDM is a retrospective interview technique, focused on exploring decision-making in its natural setting. These environments impose various challenges on the decision maker, including time pressure, high information content, and dynamic conditions (Klein et al., 1989). It is a knowledge elicitation technique for identifying and exploring operators' decision points. The selection of probes will be used to guide the investigation of users' cognitive processing.

The idea of CDM is to ask users to think about specific cases of problem-solving. While they are telling us the story of the critical incident that they have successfully handled, they are probed to discuss challenges, sources of uncertainties, and their tactics.

One particular benefit of the CDM technique is that operators are asked to describe the sequence of their activities, in response to the incident under the study. Therefore, various decision points will be identified along the way. CDM is also a good method to engage with users, as we are asking them to think of their success stories and as a result, the positive rapport between the researcher and participant will allow for a more fruitful data collection and knowledge elicitation experience (Table 4.2).

Chapter 6 reports a CDM study of maintenance control room operators to document their experiences when diagnosing and handling faults within the railways.

TABLE 4.2
CDM Based on O'Hare et al. 1998)

Probe type	Probe content
Cues	What were you seeing, hearing, smelling, etc.?
Knowledge	What information did you use in making this decision, and how was it obtained?
Analogues	Were you reminded of any previous experience?
Goals	What were your specific goals at this time?
Options	What other courses of action were considered by or available to you?
Basis	How was this option selected/other options rejected? What rule was being followed?
Experience	What specific training or experience was necessary, or helpful in making this decision?
Aiding	If the decision was not the best, what training, knowledge, or information could have helped?
Time pressure	How much time pressure was involved in making this decision? (Scales vary.)
Situation awareness	Imagine that you were asked to describe the situation to a relief officer at this point, how would you summarise the situation?
Hypotheticals	If a key feature of the situation had been different, what difference would it have made in your decision?

4.5.5 ACTIVITY ANALYSIS

Activity analysis refers to the technique that facilitates understanding people's work (Pickup et al., 2010). They provide an opportunity to explore the work conducted by operators, and the sequence of their activities and to develop an understanding of the impact of procedural change within the workplace. Activity analysis can also be used to inform cognitive characteristics of the working environment including workload and situational awareness. Chapters 6 and 7 present a detailed data collection to develop an understanding of alarm handling in railway electrical control rooms.

4.6 DATA ANALYSIS AND MODELLING

Having collected data, there is a need to structure this data in a way that expresses the nature of the work. Importantly, the outputs of the analysis should be useful to more than just the human factors expert. The outputs should be readily understandable by all stakeholders in a development, procurement, or deployment process.

4.6.1 THEMATIC CONTENT ANALYSIS

Once qualitative data is collected either through interview studies, video recording, or observation, there is a need for analysing it and making sense of the data. Thematic content analysis helps with this. Thematic content analysis (Neal and Nichols, 2001) provides an in-depth understanding of the domain from both qualitative and quantitative perspectives. It allows for exploring qualitative data (e.g., text, audio recording) in more detail. Key project goals, research questions, and objectives facilitate an understanding of relevant themes and topics. The thematic content analysis contains four stages:

- Data collection: capture data through different techniques including interview studies, document reviews, and observations
- Data collation: structure raw data to facilitate a more in-depth review (e.g., using an excel sheet)
- Theme definition classification: define specific topics of importance
- Higher order theme selection: explore the relationship between different themes and their potential association and categorisation

Thematic content analysis is a very good method to facilitate familiarisation and to define the scope of a complex problem and it has been used to analyse the interview studies described in Chapter 5.

4.6.2 SCENARIO ANALYSIS

One challenge with complex analyses of tasks and behaviour is to communicate how these concepts fit together in practice. One approach that has been used in more general usability and user-centred design is the use of scenarios (Rosson and Carrol, 2009). Scenarios are textual descriptions of how one or more people may conduct their activities. Scenarios can not only convey a series of events but also how they are shaped by context (time, location, and so on). They can be used to convey how people currently work, but also how people might work in the future. In this way they are useful to convey to design teams what the potential intended use of technology might be. Finally, scenarios can express the mainstream use of an application or software and can also be useful for describing special or "edge" cases – special cases (e.g., high-risk situations; users with specific needs, etc.). Scenarios may be particularly useful for conveying the narrative of how people work to managers and senior stakeholders, or to members of a design team. We use a scenario in Chapter 8 to show how various human factors considerations fit together when reflecting on the use of an asset management solution.

4.6.3 DECISION LADDERS

Various techniques have been presented for modelling cognitive activity during control tasks; Rasmussen's decision ladder (Rasmussen, 1986) is amongst them and is particularly useful for expressing decision-making, as the name suggests, and how this is influenced by factors such as experience, problem difficulty, and the role of automation and support.

Rasmussen (1986) listed the decision-making phases as below:

- Detection of the need for intervention
- Observe the essential data required for decision-making
- Analyse the available evidence
- Evaluate the possible consequences
- Target state is chosen through an evaluation
- Appropriate task is selected based on available resources
- The least effort requiring procedure is then selected to do the task

The decision ladder aims to identify various information processing modes. In dynamic socio-technical environments, a shift between these modes is difficult (functional fixation). These modes can be categorised into two groups: (1) information processing activities and (2) the state of knowledge resulting from information processing. This information has been shown with different symbols, to enable predictable design.

It is a template (see Figure 4.1), which frames potential cognitive states and processes within a standardised model of cognition, comprising attention, interpretation, evaluation, and decision-making, planning, and action. In most real-life

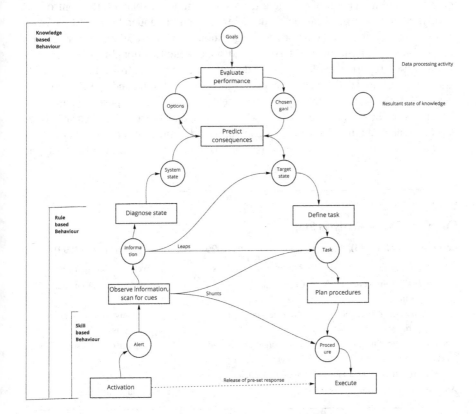

FIGURE 4.1   Template for decision ladder

decision-making situations, these phases do not actually occur, or not in such a structured way. It is mainly a framework to present the logical sequence of information processing. The decision ladder can also represent shortcuts through cognitive processing, known as shunts and leaps, therefore supporting the expression of the kind of cognitive activity that is typical of expert performance. It also enables predicting the impact of automation on cognitive processing by demonstrating the impact of interventions on specific cognitive sequences.

4.6.4 Cognitive Work Analysis

Cognitive work analysis (CWA) is a conceptual and system-based approach for analysing human information interaction in highly dynamic socio-technical workplaces (Sanderson et al., 1999; Fidel and Pejtersen, 2004). It was initially proposed by Rasmussen et al. (1994), and subsequently modified by Vicente (1999) and Lintern (2009). Table 4.3 lists the CWA stages in each of the three approaches.

CWA enables designers and developers to get a clear understanding of the work domain and to specify its functionalities. It is particularly useful when designers want to introduce new technologies to support existing cognitive functions. For example, the case that was studied in the electrical control room (ECR) (Chapter 7) informed the implication of adding a fourth information display on the controllers' workstations. However, it can be used to obtain a general understanding of an existing system as well. Human factor specialists should conduct CWA and work closely with the general engineer to understand and specify the functionalities.

ISO 11064 reports five phases of the design life cycle of control centres as clarification, analysis and definition, concept design, detailed design, and operational feedback. CWA can support some aspects of these phases, and the purpose of using CWA is that it describes "what goes on" or "what should go on" in a system in a structured and repeatable manner. Done well it can support decisions in the systems development process over who performs a task (allocation of function), people's support

---

TABLE 4.3

Cognitive Work Analysis Stages

Rasmussen et al. (1994)	Vicente (1999)	Lintern (2009)
Work domain analysis	Work domain analysis	Work domain analysis
Activity analysis in work domain terms	Control task analysis	Work organisation analysis
Activity analysis in decision-making terms	Strategies analysis	Cognitive transformation analysis
Activities analysis in terms of mental strategies	Social organisation and cooperation analysis	Cognitive processing analysis
Analysis of work organisation	Worker competencies analysis	
Analysis of system users		Social transaction analysis

needs (such as information), the loading on them, where human-centred automation can have benefits, and design of the information displays. An important aspect of CWA is that it is formative rather than prescriptive, so it can address unpredicted events or system states. It also facilitates an in-depth understanding of the context as well as the hierarchy of tasks and information that supports them. The early stages of CWA provide the designer with an overview of the system where design constraints can be easily detected (this is similar to the clarification phase in ISO 11064).

CWA has already been used in a number of rail contexts including signalling (Millen et al., 2011), train driving (Jansson et al., 2006), and engineering and track worker protection (Golightly et al., 2010).

In practice, developing a CWA takes considerable time and commitment on the part of the HF practitioner and the wider development team. Nonetheless, its holistic description of work, and the factors that shape work in a given domain, makes it a powerful approach.

CWA has been applied to system design; however, most of the work is focused on the initial stages of the CWA framework, such as Work Domain Analysis (WDA) and Abstraction Hierarchy (AH) (Groppe et al., 2009; Reising and Sanderson, 1998). Full detail of CWA and its implementation and implications are discussed in Chapter 7 of this book.

4.7 CHAPTER SUMMARY

This chapter presents key methods that can be used to inform complex socio-technical systems. A combined view of understanding context and exploring sequences of activities has been proposed, and select techniques to target each of these aspects are briefly presented. The next part of this book will present the utilisation of these methods in different rail control settings. We start with a study of maintenance activity in Chapter 5.

5 Understanding Cognition within Maintenance Contexts

5.1 CHAPTER OVERVIEW

Chapters 1–4 have introduced remote condition monitoring, the human challenges, and the human factors methods and approaches that can address these challenges. This chapter goes to the next stage by investigating some typical work contexts where maintenance monitoring technologies are used. In doing so, we will explore the role of maintenance control and different types of control rooms, including different types of automation. Reviewing the context of maintenance control provides insights regarding the difficulty of fault management (e.g., false alarms, uncertainty of diagnosis) and, consequently, the areas for improvement with future technology. This is all explored within the context of railway infrastructure monitoring.

5.2 BACKGROUND

Technological advances, including RCM systems, are commonly used within railways to enhance operators' situation awareness, decision-making, and fault finding. As discussed in Chapter 3, one of the main challenges facing multi-agent control systems is to achieve an effective understanding of how information is processed and applied.

Technology adoption and efficient utilisation of asset monitoring is dependent on careful alignment with operators' mental models, their expectations, needs, and available resources. This involves uncovering the operator's major strategies including how they perceive their roles, their situational awareness of different events/incidents, and on what basis they prioritise and make decisions. Many of these strategies indicate the important constraints that shape the way operators work and must be reflected in any future technology.

Three environments were selected to explore this variation reflecting different local conditions and legacy systems available both in terms of control equipment and rail infrastructure.

- The first was focused on the performance of key railway service assets (i.e., signals and point machines). This is relatively local, and the maintenance control comprised of a workstation located within a signal box responsible for regulating rail traffic (maintenance location A).

DOI: 10.1201/9781315587288-5

- The second location was more integrated and focused on a larger area of coverage covering both service-related infrastructures and railway assets such as buildings and power boxes (maintenance location B).
- The third type of maintenance control focused on a region within the railway network and monitored both service-related infrastructure and assets, as well as weather-related conditions that impact the state of the assets (e.g., wind gust and ice). Reflecting the strategic nature of this environment, operators were co-located with the train operator company's representatives, regulators, and maintenance technicians (maintenance location C).

The next step is therefore to look in detail at how people perform their current work – to understand the realities of their pressures and decisions. There is benefit in looking across different control settings, as it allows us to pull out regularities in how operators handle maintenance control – strategies, decisions, and requirements – irrespective of local conditions.

5.3   APPROACH

The diversity of activities in railway maintenance, and the highly cognitive nature of the work, can impose a severe challenge for understanding the work of the operators, and designing effective systems. Operators often have a sequential, rule-based approach towards certain sources of information. Presenting this information in a cohesive way that matches operators' mental models and cognitive processing is essential for designing effective decision aids.

Rasmussen and Lind (1982) specified that the route to an in-depth understanding of control settings is through investigating an operator's activities rather than reviewing system requirements. A combination of sequential and contextual data collection and analysis should be conducted to ensure that diverse nuances of human behaviour working with control environments are understood and reflected in design (Bainbridge, 1997).

A series of data collection and analysis activities were therefore used to tackle the research questions explored in this study, capturing both contextual and sequential aspects of maintenance fault finding. Figure 5.1 summarises these research activities and their outputs.

The approach used a combination of observation, informal interview studies, and field study, coupled with a more structured knowledge elicitation activity. This knowledge elicitation was informed by the critical decision method (CDM) (Klein, 1989; O'Hare et al., 1998). Participants were asked to recall a recent, challenging fault-finding incident but then were asked to consider each incident in terms of four stages. These four stages are based on models of alarm handling (Stanton, 2006) and are shown in Figure 5.2.

Given that one of the stated aims of the study was to compare different working contexts, a structure was needed to describe decision-making in each environment

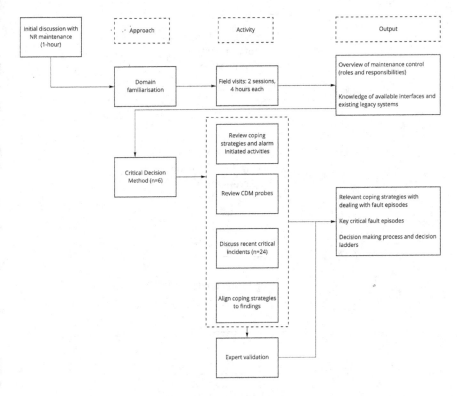

FIGURE 5.1   Research framework and methods

and compare it across settings. The lens for this work was Rasmussen's decision ladder (1986), as described in Chapter 4. While this is a component of Cognitive Work Analysis (Vicente, 1999), it predates CWA and can be used as a representational form in its own right allowing us to describe (and therefore contrast) decision-making processes.

Finally, factors such as time pressure or gaps in information can lead to the operator applying coping strategies. This is an expression of the need to balance thoroughness of analysis, with efficiency (Hollnagel, 2012). This trade-off is exacerbated when information is either incomplete/insufficient or the operator is overwhelmed by information. Also, operators are likely to be human (for the foreseeable future) with cognitive biases, for example in their ability to interpret cumulative probabilities or in their assessment of risk (Costello and Watts, 2014; Sundh and Julsin, 2018). These factors lead to a set of coping strategies. Hollnagel and Woods (2005) propose a taxonomy of typical coping strategies (see Table 5.1). These strategies allow the operator to deal with different volumes and quality of information. Therefore, a step in the analysis was to apply these strategies to the observed and described processes of fault finding.

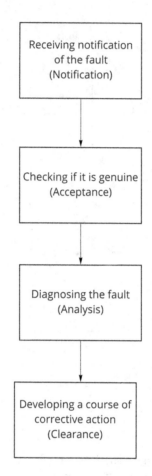

FIGURE 5.2   Four stages of fault finding according to Stanton (2006)

5.4   METHOD

5.4.1   DOMAIN FAMILIARISATION

A series of field observations, open structured interviews, and workshops were conducted to facilitate familiarisation with various types of maintenance control centres. This included the understanding of existing remote condition monitoring technologies that are currently in use within railways. Details of the main responsibilities, shift work settings, and a brief description of fault analysis processes in these control rooms were collected.

To start, a 1-hour interview was conducted with a senior railway operator to facilitate the identification of various types of railway maintenance control centres and to categorise these in terms of geographical coverage and types of equipment. Three different types of the control room were selected on the basis of these

TABLE 5.1

Coping Strategy Taxonomy from Hollnagel and Woods (2005)

Strategy	Overload/Insufficient information	Definition
Omission	Overload	Temporary, arbitrary non-processing of information is lost
Reduced precision	Overload	Trading precision for speed and time, all input is considered, but only superficially; reasoning is shallower
Queuing	Overload	Delaying response during high load, on the assumption that it will be possible to catch up later (stacking input)
Filtering	Overload	Neglecting to process certain categories; non-processed information is lost
Cutting categories	Overload	Reduce the level of discrimination and use fewer grades or categories to describe input
Decentralisation	Overload	Distributing processing if possible; calling in assistance
Escape	Overload	Abandoning the task, giving up completely, leaving the field
Extrapolation	Insufficient information	Existing evidence is "stretched" to fit a new situation; extrapolation is usually linear and is often based on fallacious causal reasoning
Frequency gambling	Insufficient information	The frequency of occurrence of past items/events is used as a basis for recognition/selection
Similarity matching	Insufficient information	The subjective similarity of past to present items/events is used as a basis for recognition/selection
Trial and error (random selection)	Insufficient information	Interpretations and/or selection does not follow any systematic principles
Laissez-faire	Insufficient information	An independent strategy is given up in lieu of just doing what others do

recommendations. These control rooms, although similar in terms of their job specifications and responsibilities, had different technologies that were also distributed in different configurations. These control rooms were selected based on the amount and type of RCM equipment they have and are referred to as locations A, B, and C throughout this chapter.

A document review was also conducted. This covered specifications of the RCM equipment, procedural manuals, and roles and responsibilities of maintenance technicians. The initial input from the senior railway operator was followed by three field visits of 4 hours each (total of 12 hours) conducted in the three maintenance control centres. This involved general observation of activities and unstructured discussions with operational staff regarding tasks, priorities, and the nature of maintenance work.

5.4.2 CRITICAL DECISION METHOD

5.4.2.1 Participants

Maintenance technicians at each location (A, B, and C) were approached with the proposed study aims and invited to participate. Two maintenance technicians from each of the selected maintenance control centres (MCC) participated in this study (n = 6). Participants were all male with an average age of 43 years, an average of 22 years of experience in various sectors of the railway, and they were all experienced at the task under observation. Interviewing six participants from the three maintenance control rooms took approximately 12 hours.

5.4.2.2 Procedure

Ethical guidelines of the University of Nottingham were followed with approval from the University of Nottingham's Faculty of Engineering Ethics Committee. Participants were assured about data confidentiality and their anonymity.

Participants were asked to think of the most recent challenging fault situations they had gone through. These incidents were selected by participants as critical or challenging ones. Therefore, as well as informing the steps of decision-making, the choices of participants also provided an insight into their perception of what constitutes a challenging fault analysis situation.

The incident was then reviewed using a set of probes based on the CDM (O'Hare et al., 1998). Each of the four stages for fault handling (notification, acceptance, analysis, and clearance) was discussed, using any of the following probes, as appropriate:

1. How did you become aware of the fault? What was the cue in the identification of the problem?
2. What was the most important piece of information that helped you in making your decision?
3. How certain were you regarding the information provided to you?
4. How did you integrate all different sources of information to come to a conclusion?
5. What artefacts did you use?
6. In what order did you attend to various pieces of information?
7. How aware were you regarding your surroundings as well as the fault's context?

Once a given fault episode was completed, the process was repeated until the time available with each participant ended. Typically, this resulted in four faults per participant. Therefore, a total of 24 fault episodes were recorded.

Due to the interviews being conducted in a live operational environment, data was not audio recorded, but contemporaneous notes were taken using an analysis spreadsheet, discussed below.

5.4.2.3   Analysis

A decision analysis spreadsheet was developed to assist with grouping and structuring the functions of fault analysis with factors adopted from the CDM (O'Hare et al., 1998). Table 5.2 shows an example of a completed spreadsheet for one of the fault analysis cases. The four stages of fault analysis are presented in the "goals/activities" column. Additional notes and comments on design recommendations were also recorded for each alarm-handling stage and further reviewed.

Participants' comments regarding questions covering what the most important piece of information was, how certain were they regarding the information provided to them, and how did they integrate all sources of information to a conclusion provided cues as to the strategies they use to overcome information deficiencies. These were then mapped to the list of coping strategies adopted from Hollnagel and Woods (2005) presented in Table 5.1. A separate 1-hour-long meeting with one of the maintenance technicians in the control room at location A was used to verify and reconfirm the identified strategies.

Further analysis examined the differences in terms of activities and strategies in relation to the type of artefacts and system distribution available in each control room. Decision ladders developed for each of the control rooms provided a means for comparing activities and strategies in each of the control rooms. Activities and strategies were first compared in terms of the available artefacts in each control room and then compared in terms of the distribution of maintenance workstations within its larger control setting.

5.5   RESULTS

5.5.1   Functional Overview

Observation and discussion with staff confirmed the basic principles and processes associated with railway maintenance and their associated environments. These are facilities with responsibility for maintaining the railway infrastructure. This ranges from maintenance of signalling and telecommunication facilities to electrical and buildings as well as track-borne infrastructure (e.g., point machines, track circuits). In Great Britain (GB), asset monitoring involved various existing systems. This variation is partially rooted in regional investments and traffic-related needs of various locations. Figure 5.3 shows an example of an operator workstation. The three maintenance control rooms associated with the present study are described in Table 5.3.

5.5.2   Fault Management Processes

The maintenance technician, also sometimes known as a flight engineer or fault controller, is responsible for detecting and dealing with operational failures, attending to fault logs, monitoring equipment to facilitate predictive maintenance, and planning periodic and long-term maintenance checks. They support the railway service and provide aid to operational staff. In doing so, there are situations where maintenance

TABLE 5.2

Example of a Completed Decision Analysis Spreadsheet

Fault type	Activities/goals	Cue identification	Data processing	Information development	Knowledge integration	Notes	Design implications
Point failure – example of promptness of fault	Get informed of the fault	Signaller (located in the same room) informed the maintenance technician that he has lost detection	The information obtained from the signaller	According to fault information the operator is aware of the location, time and brief indication of the fault. Also, he knows about the weather condition on the day	They need to assess whether that is a genuine alarm or not	This was the most important piece of information; in a way, the operator relies on the judgement of the signaller	Identifying external effectors that contribute to faults. Maybe presenting them on display will cause clutter but can allocate specific training to them
	Check if the alarm is genuine	Manually controlling the point is not possible so it is a genuine fault	Signaller's alert and failed manual control	Same as above	Needs to assess the fault now through proprietary system		
	Diagnose	Look into the normal voltage and current available on the proprietary system	Weather conditions, and status of the voltage and current	Same as above plus knowledge obtained from the proprietary system	Think of a corrective plan	Having historical data associated with the location and the weather helps	

(Continued)

TABLE 5.2 (CONTINUED)
Example of a Completed Decision Analysis Spreadsheet

Fault type	Activities/goals	Cue identification	Data processing	Information development	Knowledge integration	Notes	Design implications
	Course of action	Historical information, the evidence matches previous cases when considering external effectors	All of the information is integrated to come up with a solution which is to send out the fault team to investigate it	Same as above	Same as above	The operator not only sends the fault team out but has some clue about what is wrong there as well	The question is, whether the fault team knows that technicians had this hunch? In other words, does in any way this knowledge gets transferred to the fault team

FIGURE 5.3 Maintenance workstation in Maintenance Control Centre at location C (National Control Centre)

TABLE 5.3

The Three Maintenance Control Rooms of the Present Study

Maintenance control location	A	B	C
Type	Signalling maintenance	Signalling maintenance	National control centre
Location	Local (in the same room as the signaller)	Local (in the same room as the signaller)	Central (route control)
RCM	1 – Infrastructure event log	1 – Asset monitoring 2 – Track monitoring 3 – Point condition monitoring	1 – Wheel monitoring 2 – Track monitoring 3 – Point monitoring 4 – Weather monitoring 5 – Asset monitoring 6 – Train monitoring

technicians need to go to the site of a specific asset and locate asset-related information from the adjacent loggers and sensors.

When a fault is being reported, various types of information are presented to the operator: location, equipment type, and a brief indication of the fault. These may also occur as alarms within the maintenance control room to notify the operator of an infrastructure malfunction or abnormality. Logbooks are also used to record the following information: the date, the technician who had attended to the fault, fault management system (FMS) number, equipment type (e.g., point machine, main signal, position light signal) and equipment ID, controller unit, field unit, indication of a common fault (e.g., lamp failure, lost reverse detection, earth alarm), and common fix (e.g., filter unit replaced), as well as the current status of that fault (fixed, active, unknown, or cleared on own). Finally, a more detailed description of each fault can be found in the report that is automatically generated.

The operators then assess the fault through their asset monitoring equipment and re-play the asset behaviour towards the moment of its failure and diagnose the fault. Often operators would require further information in order to build a mental image of the situation that led to the failure. This is then followed by sending a specialised track team to the field to rectify the failure and resume normal service. During this process, maintenance controllers are in communication with signallers, route managers, and other operational staff to develop and share a good understanding of the impact of the failure on the service.

5.5.3 Maintenance Control Contexts

These maintenance control rooms had various ranges of condition monitoring equipment. The comparison of these three provided insights into how operators cope and adapt to the technological innovations that were being added to their existing control environments. It is interesting to note that the scope and high-level activities and roles of these maintenance operators are quite similar. The main difference was due to the geographical location, area of coverage, and more importantly the technological capabilities that have become available to operators in each of these maintenance locations.

Workstation at Location A had seven information displays. Artefacts available to the maintenance technicians included equipment linked to various fault monitoring and remote condition monitoring systems for monitoring the state of point machines and track circuits based on data from on-track sensors and loggers. Some of these interfaces were web-based, while others comprised stand-alone software applications. Systems available to the technicians had different interfaces that were not always consistent in terms of their basic presentation. Apart from the use of similar colour coding (e.g., red for alarms and green for cleared), the format for information presentation differed between different interfaces. In addition to the condition monitoring facilities, signalling displays of the area under coverage and Control Centre of the Future (CCF) (a wide area view of the regional network) were also available to the signalling technicians.

The control room at location A only had logging facilities equipped with alarms to notify the maintenance operator when the logged value was above a certain threshold. Additionally, since the technicians were located in the same signal box as the signaller, they could overhear relevant information and this, in turn, formed another source of their information when it came to identifying the occurrence of a failure.

Workstation at Location B consisted of six information displays. These included five integrated information displays and one display used for web-based applications, as well as the administrative tasks that the maintenance technician needed to fulfil as part of their duties. The information displays on the workstation provided information regarding signalling workstations, power supply, monitoring facilities for the office equipment, modems, and other communication links. Location B had some predictive monitoring capability, but the system only covered local assets. These provided operators with detailed trends and graphs associated with the fault that were used when diagnosing faults.

Workstation at Location C consisted of nine displays. These covered various asset types, point monitoring, and wheel monitoring, but also a rich range of contextual information including weather monitoring and train schedules. A display was also dedicated to e-mail and other information resources. Location C not only had many predictive monitoring solutions but also covered a large geographical area. This technology provided diagnostic support, assisting operators in a more confident acceptance of the fault. The wide range of RCM equipment in the control room provided operators with duplicated information which could be beneficial in supporting diagnoses, though in some cases generated excessive information.

5.5.4 Fault Analysis Using Critical Decision Method

A total of 24 fault analysis episodes were recorded and analysed using the CDM technique – 9 of these fault analysis episodes were recorded in location A, 9 in location B, and 7 in location C.

From the 24 cases of fault finding, 13 different types of faults were selected by maintenance technicians. These faults are perceived by the operators to be the most recurring and challenging cases. False alarms, point failures, and signal failures were selected more than other cases. The distribution of fault types is shown in Figure 5.4.

These faults are selected by technicians due to both their frequency (i.e., false alarm is a constant occurrence) and their severity (i.e., point and signal failures can seriously impact the service [Golightly and Dadashi, 2017]). The fault process can be summarised across the four stages as follows:

Notification – when a fault is reported, the operator is made aware of it. As well as getting alerted through another controller and audible and visual channels, the operator also has to identify the location from which the fault has originated and needs to start analysing the faulty situation on the basis of their local knowledge and experience.

Acceptance – the second stage is to identify whether the fault is genuine or not. This is to assess the credibility of the data presented. If the maintenance in the control room has been alerted to a signalling or points failure

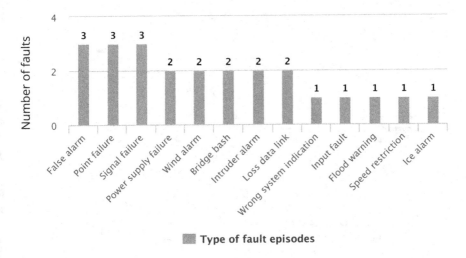

Type of fault episodes

FIGURE 5.4 Number of the faults reviewed in the study

by someone else, it is not a false alarm. If they have received an RCM alert, then they need to explore the alarm further. If the fault is not genuine and the operator imposes an unnecessary speed restriction or even stops a train to send an investigation team to the track, this can lead to unnecessary delays and a waste of time and resources, as well as excess costs in terms of delay attribution fines.

Analysis – the third stage of fault analysis is to assess the fault, seek potential causes of the fault, and diagnose it.

Clearance – finally, the fourth stage refers to the development and evaluation of the optimum corrective action.

Nineteen of the fault cases followed this basic process. In the remaining five cases, where the technician was not completely certain whether the fault was authentic or not, a test of authenticity was performed and, in two of the cases where there was a false alarm, the technician assessed the causes associated with the generation of a false alarm. In these five cases, upon confirming the authenticity of the fault episode, the cause was diagnosed, and a corrective course of action was selected.

5.5.5 Decision Ladders

A canonical decision ladder was developed representing the basic process of fault identification and analysis in location A. This is shown in Figure 5.5, with the transition between incoming notification of a fault through to acceptance and analysis and planning a course of action. These four areas are circled in the figure.

One of the research questions in this study was whether changes in the artefacts and equipment available to operators would affect the process of fault analysis. The data obtained from the CDM interviews informed three decision ladders. The

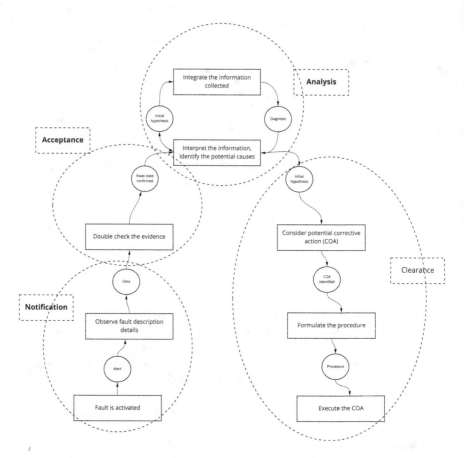

FIGURE 5.5   Decision ladder for fault analysis in the control room at location "A"

decision ladders of fault analysis in locations "B" and "C" are shown in Figure 5.6 and Figure 5.7, respectively.

The shaded areas in Figure 5.6 and 5.7 refer to the activities that are being assisted through the artefacts available in those control rooms. Although the workstation at location "A" had no noticeable support from any advanced equipment in their room, "B" and "C" used various technologies to diagnose faults and assist the investigation process. The second stage (confirmation) and the third stage (diagnosis) benefitted from increased analytical support. Most notably, at workstations "A" and "B" when operators wanted to check if the fault is genuine, they applied their knowledge of the fault location and the history of that asset. In the control room at location "C", operators had more trust in the system, potentially because the equipment had been maintained more regularly and alarm thresholds had been updated fairly recently. The sophisticated nature of fault management systems, and the strategic nature of the role of operators in this control room, contributed to this difference.

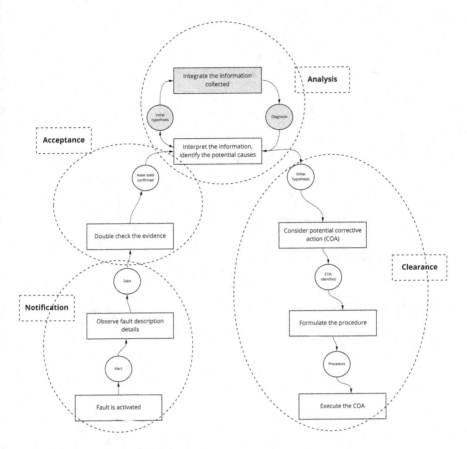

FIGURE 5.6 Decision ladder for fault analysis in the control room at location "B"

5.5.6 STRATEGIES

Both the familiarisation studies and the CDM interview findings identified regular strategies and tactics applied by maintenance operators. Comments recorded during the CDM study were assessed against Hollnagel and Woods' (2005) coping strategies (Table 5.1). Table 5.4 shows participants' responses to the questions for the selection of fault analysis episodes, with probes around cues and information seeking being particularly relevant to uncovering strategies.

Deficiencies in information presentation were one of the main challenges facing the participants endeavouring to deal optimally with faults. There were at least six information displays on a technician's workstation. The same data being available on multiple existing systems contributed to unnecessarily redundant information and misleading data. Additionally, temporal aspects associated with handling alarms often meant that technicians did not have sufficient time to exhaustively search for information to handle the fault effectively. Hence, they were selected as representative cases for the CDM.

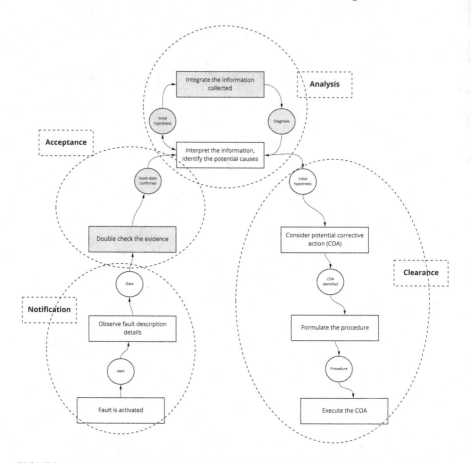

FIGURE 5.7   Decision ladder for fault analysis in the control room at location "C"

The seven faults listed in Table 5.4 are identified by participants as being challenging due to some form of information deficiency and therefore would be appropriate candidates to explore operator's strategies when dealing with information deficiencies. Strategies are presented in parentheses. The strategies adopted by maintenance technicians to analyse the faults include categorising, filtering, queuing, similarity matching, and extrapolation. However, participants also tend to use the frequency of occurrence of events in the past as a basis for recognition (frequency gambling). Many of these strategies (categorising, filtering, and queuing) were in response to the high number of alarms that were generated, sometimes by the same fault, and as a means of managing tasks. Similarity matching, extrapolation and frequency gambling were more relevant to the interpretation of events in particular to assess whether the alarm was genuine.

When comparing the three control environments, locations "A" and "B" showed similar strategies, though participants at location "B" did not need to do as much "filtering" and "categorising" since their more advanced condition monitoring systems

TABLE 5.4

Examples of Technicians' Responses to the Three Questions about a Selection of Faults

Fault	What was the most important piece of information that helped you in recognising the fault?	How certain you were regarding the information provided to you?	How did you integrate all sources of information and come to a conclusion?
1	I know there is engineering work in Manchester Piccadilly (similarity matching).	We heard about the power shutdown in Manchester Piccadilly earlier (extrapolation).	Used the diagnostic tools on the fault management system to confirm my assumptions (categorising).
2	Signaller located in the same control room informed me that they may have lost detection (categorising).	I double-checked the point on responsiveness on my system and I trust the signaller's call (filtering).	The weather was icy on that day and I decided that it was weather related (extrapolation).
3	Alarm description on the banner (filtering).	I know the specific location where this alarm happens; if it's the same location, it confirms it (similarity matching).	I look at the backup copy from the system and filter the potential causes (filtering).
4	The red fault on the display of the fault management system (filtering).	The power supply is showing unexpected behaviour; other related alarms are being generated (similarity matching).	Filter and categories relevant information on the fault management system (categorising and filtering).
5	Unusual fault in the fault management system (extrapolation).	Engineering has just changed the module which is alarming (similarity matching).	Eliminate all possible options to reach a conclusion (filtering).
6	Signalling screenshots, it went red all the way, it was really difficult to miss (filtering).	Again, having the signaller in the same room was really helpful, also this is the Signal Passed at Danger alarm which is very critical, you really don't think twice (categorising).	I rang other signallers in other control rooms to get a bigger picture, everything was alright towards Manchester and was not alright towards Crewe (filtering).
7	This location and this specific fault happen all the time and I know from previous cases, that they are all false alarms (similarity matching).	90% of the stuff shown on these fault management systems is false alarms (frequency gambling).	I would have to find a way to send a fault team on track to check if the equipment is working (filtering).

helped with searching and grouping faults. However, they still used "extrapolation" and "similarity matching" when it came to identifying and assessing whether the fault was genuine at the "acceptance" stage. At location "C", operations were more centralised, and operators had access both to more information and more advanced analytics, removing the need for "filtering" and "categorising". The key aspects of the faults are clear and unambiguous. Also, because there was sufficient integration of information, operators in location "C" had to resort to less "extrapolation" to fill too many gaps in their interpretation of a fault. However, operators still engaged in "similarity matching" by recalling a similar scenario to diagnose the fault and an appropriate course of action.

5.6   DISCUSSION

The study reported in this chapter aimed to shed light on the cognitive work of rail maintenance controllers. In terms of the nature of the maintenance role, the results suggest maintenance is a cognitive task, adhering to conventional models of alarm/fault handling, and reliant on different levels of automation which play an increasing role. What is less expected is the variation in the role depending on location and scope of functions, though this matches the similar experience of rail signalling (Pickup et al., 2013). The analysis clearly suggests that local conditions and needs, both in the maintenance control box and for the infrastructure covered, are an important factor when reflecting on the nature of work. It is also interesting that "active overhearing" and the ability to work with others are an advantage in some of these environments (location A). This suggests a team – and distributed – rather than purely individual, orientation to the work.

One interesting aspect of the analysis is the selection of faults that were identified by the operators during the CDM interviews. Participants were asked to remember the cases that were particularly challenging during this knowledge elicitation (Table 5.2), and their selection is a glimpse into what operators perceived as the most recurring or challenging cases. False alarms, point failures, and signal failures were selected more than in other cases. These faults affect the immediate operation of the railways, and operators found them more challenging, possibly due to the time pressure felt while analysing these fault situations. It is worth noting that a study of signallers and controllers in rail disruption (Golightly and Dadashi, 2017) also identified point and signal failures as among the most challenging events, due to the wide-ranging causes and the need for extended diagnosis.

It seems that, in most instances, operators did not have a clear view of the fault (e.g., due to the lost communication between the sensor and the logger in "lost data link"), while, in other instances, they had too much information to analyse. Support for these cases would appear to be an area where there could be a significant gain for operations. It is therefore the case that these events are worth special attention, both cognitively, in terms of high-quality sensing and algorithms, and in terms of HMI.

Data collected about fault analysis episodes suggest that the second stage (confirmation) and the third stage (diagnosis) benefit from advanced technologies which can take on cognitive load. In both locations "A" and "B", when operators wanted to check if the fault is genuine, they used their knowledge of the faulty location and the history of that asset. In location "C" operators had more trust in the system, potentially because of the sophistication of the fault management systems and the strategic nature of the role of operators in this control room. It highlights that maintenance fault finding is a complex set of activities, and that human judgement and machine intelligence are tightly connected, rather than independent (Hollnagel and Woods, 2005). Being able to reflect this complex process in the form of a decision ladder which includes both humans and automation as a single cognitive system will allow designers to consider this process more holistically in future.

A review of the strategies adopted by operators during fault-finding episodes revealed that "filtering", "similarity matching", and "categorising" are, respectively, the most utilised coping strategies when facing information deficiencies, particularly in those scenarios where responding to a fault is time critical and where thoroughness must be traded off against efficiency (Hollnagel, 2012). Those points where coping strategies are applied indicate where automation may offer significant benefits. It also suggests that the design of the HMI should support these functions and, similar to Golightly et al. (2018), rather than a black box of "red", "amber", and "green", the automation should support the exploration of the reasoning behind decisions so that both the cause and potential rectifying action can be understood.

Finally, in terms of applying methods that combine contextual and sequential approaches, this chapter showcases the possibility of developing and understanding cognitive capabilities and strategies using a relatively simple knowledge elicitation technique but triangulated together. One of the key strengths of the method was to gain input from a senior member of staff early in the process. This not only identified the right (and varied) locations to perform the work, but it also led to significant buy-in from the staff involved in the observation and the CDM.

It is appreciated that obtaining an in-depth understanding of strategies used for problem-solving requires far more detailed and extended data collection than merely finding a pattern through a number of questions. However, these data are useful in developing a general view of operators' potential approaches to overcome complications while they are attending to a fault.

5.7 CHAPTER SUMMARY

Maintenance control fault finding is critical to rail performance and safety. It is also a function under change through the increasing use of automation and "Intelligent Infrastructure". The study presented in this chapter has shed light on the nature of this work, and how it varies by location and depending on the level of automation.

In the next chapter, we move on to analyse alarms in another critical domain for rail Intelligent Infrastructure – electrical control – and drill down specifically on a key aspect of maintaining control and of future Intelligent Infrastructure solutions – the handling of alarms.

6 Understanding Alarm Handling: A Case in Railway Electrical Control Systems

6.1 CHAPTER OVERVIEW

One important aspect of maintenance systems is the need to manage alarms that notify users of possible disruptions in asset performance. This chapter presents a study undertaken in an electrical control room (ECR), an environment that is critical for managing, monitoring, and maintaining the electrical supply aspects of the railways. The study set out to capture the functions and processes of alarm handling and, in particular, the application of strategies and tactics adopted by operators when handling alarms within ECRs.

The key objectives of this chapter are to:

1. Provide an in-depth description of alarm functions within rail ECRs.
2. Mapping alarm-handling strategies to stages of alarm handling to inform the design of better alarm management systems.
3. Demonstrate methodologies for use by others wishing to take an operator-centric view of the design and deployment of similar complex systems.

6.2 BACKGROUND

Faults in railway maintenance are critical but can also be time-sensitive. Asset failures can result in major disruption to business continuity or lead to critical and fatal incidents. One example is rail electrical control. Railway ECRs in Britain were originally integrated from a number of adjacent railway traction power supply systems. Since 1932, electrical control operators (ECR operators) have been responsible for remotely opening and closing electrical equipment, instructing staff on the operation of manual switches, and leading the maintenance and fault-finding of electrification distribution and equipment. Electrical control is a key strategic area for effective rail operations that's necessary to ensure a continuous supply of power to the track and thus enable rail infrastructure managers (such as Network Rail) to meet their contractual obligations to provide an effective rail network for railway undertakers such as train operating companies. Electrical control is also a safety critical area, with electrical isolation being a key part of safe access to the track during maintenance,

DOI: 10.1201/9781315587288-6

engineering, and incident handling (Golightly et al., 2013) in those parts of the rail network that use electric traction.

This chapter focuses on alarm handling in rail ECRs. Chapter 3 introduced some of the human challenges of alarms, such as their accurate interpretation and the cognitive demands of dealing with high volumes of alarms. Alarms range from simple prompts for an operator to carry out further actions to alerts containing semantically rich messages for fault diagnosis that carry verbal, textual, or pictorial information about the source or cause of abnormalities. While alarm systems are already used generally within RCM, the shift to prognostic systems will see alarms move away from reactive indications of a current or recent event (e.g., failure of an infrastructure asset), to include anticipatory alerts and proactive notifications that warn the operator of an emerging risk (e.g., potential failure or degradation of asset performance). While some of the technology has moved on since the time of the original study (around 2010), the SCADA system is being replaced with a newer system that is being rolled out across the country. The cognitive challenges remain the same in other sectors. Importantly, the methods to study this kind of work are also still relevant.

6.3   APPROACH

As noted in Chapter 5, field studies are useful for comprehensively understanding the domain (Bisantz and Drury, 2005), enabling researchers to identify significant issues in complex socio-technical settings. Sundstrom and Salvador (1995) have noted that structured field studies can interconnect with exploratory observational studies to produce an in-depth understanding of user needs. However, when operators conduct cognitive activities (i.e., remembering, monitoring, etc.), their underlying neurological processes are not visible. Observation of the responses alone is not sufficient to get a clear understanding of the activity. Verbal protocol analysis (Ericsson, 2006) facilitates the capture of these mental processes by asking the operator to "think aloud" by explaining their decision-making either while performing the tasks or following the completion of the activity (Bainbridge and Sanderson, 2005). However, unstructured verbal protocols may not access important information regarding performance or concurrent activity.

For this study, a two-stage approach was taken (Figure 6.1). Familiarisation through observations and semi-structured interviews facilitated an overview of the work domain and led to the development of an observational checklist. The observational checklist was developed from a series of open interviews with the railway electrical operators; this led to an understanding of the activities associated with alarm handling, particularly the challenges and artefacts adopted by operators during alarm management. Such checklists have been used previously in signalling control environments (Sharples et al., 2011 and Pickup et al., 2005). A second round of observations was then conducted using the observational checklist, along with verbal protocol and video recording footage of operators handling alarms, to develop a fundamental understanding of alarm handling in the ECR.

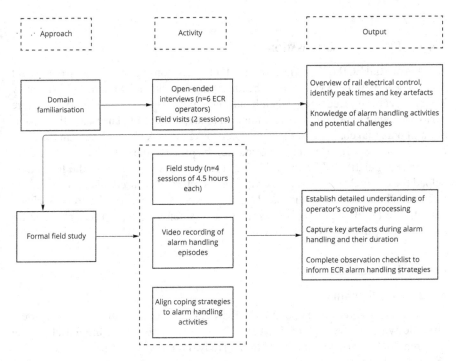

FIGURE 6.1   Approach adopted to explore alarm handling in the ECR

The combination of observational checklist data and verbal protocol enabled an analysis of frequencies and sequences of events, using a simplified version of the model developed by Stanton and Stammers (1998). This model includes two sets of events: routine and critical. When an alarm is generated, operators observe the reported warning and accept it as genuine. Operators might analyse, correct, monitor, or reset the alarm based on their understanding of a failure. If the cause of the failure is unknown, the operator will conduct a series of investigations to diagnose the problem. Finally, the operator will monitor the situation to ensure that the abnormality is dealt with (Stanton and Stammers, 1998).

The methods and results cover two strands of analysis. The first strand used observations and interviews to understand the underlying contextual factors – functions, performance criteria, alarm types, environment, and processes – of ECRs. The second strand used verbal protocols and an observational checklist to identify the sequence of activities and particular coping strategies that operators adopt during alarm-handling episodes. Together, these two sets of analyses shed light on the factors that influence alarm handling in ECRs, and the data collected went on to form a cognitive systems analysis of rail electrical control alarm handling (presented in Chapter 7).

6.4   METHOD

6.4.1   Domain Familiarisations

A Network Rail ECR (ECR A) was visited for two sessions before the setup of the field study. The aim of these visits was to become familiar with the domain and to identify key artefacts used frequently when handling alarms. Unstructured interviews were performed with ECR operators to initiate an understanding of alarm-handling activities and potential challenges. Operators were asked to talk about alarm handling and to identify issues affecting the performance, the process, the control room specifications, and regulations. Moreover, having these two sessions prior to the field study helped the researcher build rapport with the operators. It ensured that they were fully informed about the study's aims and the various stages of data collection associated with it. The familiarisation visits led to an assessment of the resources required for the field study and the design of the observational checklist.

6.4.2   Formal Field Study

6.4.2.1   Participants

Six electrical control room operators in ECR A participated in the study. They were all male with a mean age of 51 years. They were approached, briefed about the research, and agreed to participate in the study. Potential participants were briefed about the research and had the opportunity to discuss the study before giving their informed consent to take part. Participants were also assured about the issues associated with data confidentiality, anonymity, and their right to withdraw at any point during the study. Data were recorded on the basis of the number of alarms generated, not based on the individual attending to them.

6.4.2.2   Apparatus

A spreadsheet was prepared to structure the findings obtained from the field studies and to provide timeline data of the ECR operator's interaction with the control setting while alarm handling. The observational checklist was time stamped and allowed structured alarm-related activities and the use of various artefacts within specific time frames, and this enabled a sequential understanding of the alarm-handling process. Table 6.1 shows an example of the spreadsheet. This spreadsheet facilitated an understanding of the use of various artefacts used while handling an alarm. Furthermore, since the checklist was time stamped, it was possible to estimate the amount of time each artefact was used, as well as the sequence of use.

The time stamping divided each alarm-handling episode into 15-second time frames. In each time frame, the use of artefacts was assessed. For example, it was noted if, during the first 15 seconds of alarm handling, the operators were on the phone and talking to a colleague in the control room (classified as "face to face"). Measurements of the occupancy of operators with each of the artefacts provided an understanding of their importance at any given time in the alarm-handling process. The total use and the overall time used for each artefact were recorded on the

TABLE 6.1
Observational Checklist Filled for One Alarm Episode

Time	Telephone	Face to face	Alarm banner	Menu	Display area	Page button	Overview	Static board	Paper	High information	Low information
0:00:01	✓	✓								✓	
0:00:16			✓		✓	✓					
0:00:31			✓			✓	✓				
0:00:46		✓			✓			✓			
Total (seconds)	7.5	15	10		10	10	5	5			

checklist. Additionally, operators were asked to comment on the amount of information presented to them and this comment was also recorded on the spreadsheet.

Four sessions of 4.5 hours each (two day shifts and two night shifts) were planned
with the operators. The operators' activities and the use of artefacts when handling
real-time alarms (both expected and unexpected) were recorded and analysed in
detail.

During the familiarisation phase, it became apparent that operators had to deal
with two types of alarms, referred to as "expected" and "unexpected" alarms.
Maintenance procedures on the track can cause abnormalities, and, consequently, a
series of alarms will be generated in the control room. However, in these cases, the
operators are likely to be expecting the alarm, as they know the schedule and details
of the maintenance being carried out on the track. Therefore, these alarms would
not surprise the operators. This is different from cases where the operators are not
expecting the alarm, so it alerts them to a new problem.

When an alarm was generated, the researcher started the video recording and
noted the artefacts utilised during the alarm-handling episode in the observational
checklist (these observations were verified through the video recordings). When the
alarm was cleared, the operator informed the researcher that he was ready to answer
questions (retrospective verbal protocol). The researcher then annotated the observational checklist based on this information. These questions were also addressed to
explore operators coping strategies (presented in Chapter 5, Table 5.1). For example,
they would use filtering or categorising to assist with their search. The strategies
were defined and discussed with operators throughout the familiarisation phase; they
were then referred to further during the verbal protocol session in which participants
were asked to select a relevant strategy associated with the activities noted.

When no alarms were being observed, the researcher engaged in additional
discussions with the operators about their work and made observations regarding
general activities in the control room. This qualitative information from the operators helped to develop a more comprehensive understanding of activities performed
within the ECR.

6.5 FINDINGS

6.5.1 FUNCTION OVERVIEW

ECR operators have two main responsibilities; the first is to monitor the status of the
electrical supply. If there is a loss of power on the railway infrastructure, the operator is notified by the SCADA system and proceeds with the appropriate rectifying
procedure. The second function is to manage and plan the isolation of the power supply system when a maintenance team needs to work on the track. This also involves
programming the isolations and switching circuit breakers, as well as informing the
maintenance teams, the signaller controlling the area, and other stakeholders about
the status of the track and whether it is safe for track access or operational for traffic.

ECR operators communicate with signallers and inform them that the railway
tracks have electrical supplies. Moreover, they communicate with maintenance staff to

confirm that the power is isolated and that the infrastructure is safe for track workers to undertake any work on site. This is conducted through a three-way communication system to assist with the accuracy of the procedure. In three-way communication, the operator conveys a message over the phone. The recipient of the message will repeat, and then the operator will repeat one more time to confirm that the recipient has got the correct message. During major incidents (e.g., overhead line failures), this communication is extended to staff in other control rooms (including route control managers, incident controllers, and shift signaller managers) to provide information regarding the estimated time of availability of the service and to allow train running controllers and signallers to plan service recovery and train regulating and re-routing activities.

Operators are usually occupied with other activities when an alarm occurs (programming isolation work and communicating with relevant track workers regarding ongoing engineering work, etc.). The electrical control domain is highly dependent on successful alarm handling to maintain the continuity of the service while at the same time identifying spurious false alarms that are generated through testing and maintenance work or for unknown reasons.

6.5.2   Rail ECR Alarms

Rail ECR alarms are events configured in the system that require an operator's attention following any form of abnormality in the rail network's electrical supply system – for example, through Alternating Current (AC) overhead wires or Direct Current (DC) third rail. They are announced by an audible alarm and the updating of any related symbols on an alarm banner, as well as the provision of live indications on the SCADA display.

ECR A is a typical electrical control room. It has three workstations and similar information is available to all three. At the time of this study, the SCADA display in the ECR was developed on the basis of Network Rail's system specification recommendations and corresponds to EEMUA standards (EEMUA, 1999).

Two ECR operators are active at any one time and the third workstation is used for emergencies, or when extra staff are required. Of the two workstations, one of the operators is in charge and acts as a supervisor.

Figure 6.2 shows a traditional ECR operators display screen array. The left screen on the featured workstation displays the main track overview, the centre-left screen shows the DC overview, and the centre-right screen, which is used for alarm handling, contains all of the operational displays. Finally, the right screen displays the AC overview and the AC connectivity page.

These information displays contain numerous duplications which are often used as a source for confirmation by operators. For example, when there is a circuit breaker failure, the operator can compare the alterations on the AC and DC information displays to determine the extent of the failure (e.g., grid level). The operational display has the most interaction points. This is where isolations can be implemented and alarms can be explored and assessed. While the operational display is for executing operational decisions, the three remaining displays are used for providing information.

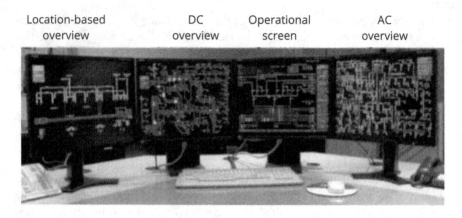

| Location-based overview | DC overview | Operational screen | AC overview |

FIGURE 6.2   ECR workstation in ECR A (UK)

Apart from dynamic information displays on their desks, there is also a static board covering one wall of the ECR. This board shows the links and platforms of the area under control. Although the board is now outdated, some of the less experienced operators use it to familiarise themselves with the area. It must be noted that this technology was towards the end of its life when the work was done. One of the features of ECR alarms is that they have been prioritised by a ranking system, with six being the lowest priority alarm and one being the highest.

Any unacknowledged alarm appears on the alarm banner, which is located on the operational display. The alarm banner can contain up to seven alarms, and if there are more than that at one time, an arrow is displayed on the right-hand side in the colour of the highest priority alarm not displayed (Figure 6.3).

Not surprisingly, operators noted availability and reliability of information as one of the challenges associated with their alarm handling. Alarms can have "high information" or "low information" associated with them. The information density can be associated with the complexity of the alarm or the overload of information associated with the event. "High information" refers to cases in which there is excessive information and the operator is overloaded (e.g., duplications of information sources). "Low information" refers to cases in which the operator does not have sufficient information to diagnose and handle the alarm. It should be noted that these terms refer to operators' subjective interpretations of the situation since it was not possible to objectively assess the sufficiency and relevancy of the information presented to operators during real-time alarm handling. Post-event verbal protocol and SME review would provide sufficient information to discover patterns. Operators know which problems are hard to diagnose and why.

Other issues that operators noted included system lag when they wanted to close circuit breakers to prepare for isolation. If there were several circuit breakers, they had to be modified sequentially since the SCADA would not allow synchronised switching. This was not the case with previous electro-mechanical mimic diagrams. Another issue was related to implementing last-minute alterations to the maintenance

Alarm banner

Menu

Display area

Page button

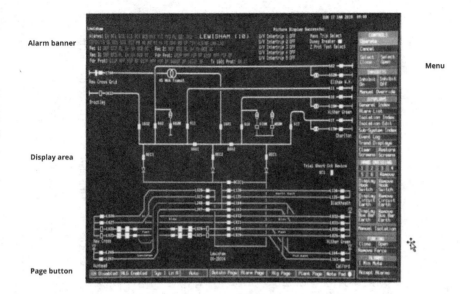

FIGURE 6.3   Operational display

plans. This would introduce additional cognitive demand since the operator had to reverse the existing isolation and permit and implement new ones within a pressured time frame.

6.5.3 ALARM-INITIATED ACTIVITIES

A review of the qualitative information collected during the verbal protocol analysis led to the identification of activities associated with alarm handling. Operators' comments were video recorded and transcribed before thematic analysis (Miles and Huberman, 1994) was undertaken. Table 6.2 presents three examples (two unexpected alarms and one expected alarm) of this coding activity.

The first stage of alarm handling is "notification", and this is the first opportunity the operator has to notice the alarm. All unacknowledged alarms appear on the alarm banner, which is located on the operational display (as shown in Figure 6.4). The information provided includes the colour of the banner and the category of alarm which roughly indicates the type of failure.

The second stage is "acceptance". This refers to the activities that are conducted by the operator to ensure that the alarm is not a false one.

Usually, alarm handling is conducted by consulting other sources of information to confirm the existence of an actual failure. In the case of expected alarms, because the operator is aware of the maintenance work that is happening in the area, they don't usually need to consult other sources. This increases the risk of misdiagnosing any unexpected alarms that are generated in the same area as other engineering works.

TABLE 6.2
Thematic Analysis of Alarm-Handling Qualitative Findings

Alarm	Notification	Acceptance	Analysis	Clearance
Unexpected	It took 3 s for the operator to look at the alarm and grab the mouse and acknowledge the alarm by clicking on the operational display.	And another 4 s to load the new page which caused the alarm. Operator explains that: "All we get is the alarm banner, we then look at the overview and grab the information and decide what is wrong, it's like second nature. When you are looking at the colour, you think what category alarm it is and you know what is the priority of each category and what are the things associated with the potential causes of the alarms based on the categories".	Operator noted that: "Once you get here it could be anything. There is no way we can tell what the problem is. But in this case it is a trip charge. It just dropped a lot of threshold and its gone back to normal now. And now 1 am checking another page to check the threshold on another location 11 and when I see that is also, it confirms my hypothesis".	"I increase the threshold and rectify the problem and then ensure that the area is covered and safe".
Unexpected	An audible siren is activated. Four seconds after that operator clicks on the alarm banner.	He says: "Looks like one of the breakers has failed", and he accepts and silences the alarm.	Four seconds after and he concludes that both of the breakers have failed, he spent another 15 s looking at the alarm and its indication to work out what is the problem. He opens the event log and tries to find the breakers on the screen and then go through the events. He reviews the facts presented on the event log.	He then tries to close the circuit breaker, but the system is not very responsive, and he uses a shortcut on the system to close down the breakers.
Expected	"There are multiple alarms, but that is just because 1 set the testing like that".	"Then because 1 know what it is, 1 accept the alarm".	"I know exactly what has caused this alarm, but also from reviewing of the alarm categories my expectation is confirmed".	"I correct the fault through SCADA and log the event".

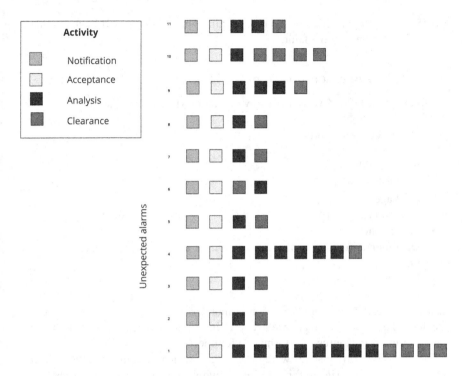

FIGURE 6.4 Order of alarm-handling activities for unexpected alarms

The third stage, "analysis", consists of the process that is conducted by the operator to analyse and diagnose the cause (or causes) of the failure and to investigate potential corrective actions. Operators explore situational information including previous faults reported at the location, recent engineering work, the status of the service (i.e., peak time/off-peak), and the availability of maintenance staff to access the faulty area and perform diagnostic investigation.

The last stage is "clearance". This refers to a series of activities conducted to select the optimum corrective action. Optimum in this context would relate to a "smart" way of dealing with the faulty situation. For example to know which maintenance team is closer to the failure site or to inform the route control managers with an accurate estimated time of availability and facilitate better coordination between different teams. Operators should consider the impact of the failure on the safety and efficiency of the service, plan the corrective action (i.e., when to send electrical technicians on track), and inform relevant parties (e.g., signallers) of the fault. Note must be taken that clearance does not refer to complete rectification of the failure but indicates that a plan has been established to rectify it.

Operators commented that one of their key challenges was to focus on alarms while they were fully occupied with other responsibilities. This was particularly the case during peak times when the operator needed to maintain the service without compromising safety. Additionally, during night shifts, operators commented on the risk of overlooking a situation due to presuming that it was caused by maintenance work rather than a genuine fault.

6.5.4   USE OF ARTEFACTS DURING ALARM HANDLING

The following artefacts were utilised by operators while alarm handling:

- SCADA display features
   a. Menu
   b. Alarm banner
   c. Display area
   d. Page buttons
   e. Overview display
- Static board
- Documentation (e.g., forms, isolation plans, reference material, etc.)
- Phone
- Face-to-face communication

Although face-to-face communication is more of a social activity than a physical one, it has been considered an artefact here since this form of communication represents an important source of information for operators.

In total, 22 alarm episodes were observed; of which 11 were unexpected and 11 were expected (e.g., triggered by testing or maintenance). Completion of the observation checklist allowed an estimation of the degree to which various displays were used during episodes of alarm management. For example, in 1 episode captured, 12 uses of different information displays and other artefacts were noted.

Furthermore, operators were asked to identify the alarm types as "high information" and "low information". It must be noted that only unexpected alarms were considered for this categorisation. From the total of 11 unexpected alarm episodes, 6 were categorised as high information and 5 were categorised as low information alarms.

Looking through the duration, mean and standard deviation (SD) of the expected and unexpected alarms it was not surprising to see that the duration of handling unexpected alarms (Mean = 78.42 s and SD = 39.07 s) was higher than the duration of handling expected alarms (Mean = 41.57 s and SD = 11.40 s). The utilisation of various artefacts during expected and unexpected alarms showed that the management of unexpected alarms resulted in the use of a "display area" as the primary information source (37% of the total duration of alarm handling). Operators use the alarm banner (8%) and telephone (8%) when handling alarms during expected alarms. This is not surprising as, during unexpected alarms, the operators need to conduct investigations before diagnosis. In contrast, they are possibly on the phone with the maintenance team during expected alarms and clear the alarm by clicking on the alarm banner.

In order to investigate the differences in the use of artefacts between high information (M = 0.38, SD = 0.49) and low information (M = 0.84, SD = 0.37), an independent samples t-test was applied. The results revealed that the display area attendance is significantly higher in alarms with high information; t (59) = −3.63, p < 0.01. The use of telephones and the display area were found to be significantly different, depending on the type of alarm. There was a significant difference between the number of times operators used the telephone in unexpected (M = 0.131, SD = 0.340) and expected conditions (M = 0.592, SD = 0.050); t (86) = −5.044, p < 0.01. Also, there was a significant difference between the number of times operators interacted with the display area in unexpected (M = 0.524, SD = 0.503) and expected (M=0.222, SD = 0.423) conditions; t (86) = 2.721, p < 0.01.

6.5.5   Use of Artefacts during Alarm Handling

Operators viewed Table 5.1 (the list of coping strategies, presented in Chapter 5) prior to the retrospective verbal protocol and were asked to identify their coping strategies during the alarm-handling episodes. The coping strategies identified were:

- Queuing
- Filtering and categorising
- Similarity matching
- Extrapolation
- Trial and error

These strategies were adopted at different stages of an alarm-handling episode. The time-stamped observational checklist facilitated the correspondence of the alarm-initiated activities to the selected coping strategies.

Operators noticed the alarm from various information sources. These included: the flashing alarm banner, colour codes, acronyms of alarm type and location, sirens, phone calls, and a flashing circle around the location on the overview display. Operators had to *categorise* and *filter* these sources to achieve a basic understanding of the alarm. In the case of multiple alarms, operators *queued* them based on their experience. Queuing often depended on the type of alarm and the location of the failed asset to identify potential impacts on the service. The prioritisation was mainly based on ensuring safety and reducing delays to the railway service.

In the rare cases of an alarm where immediate onsite action was required, operators used their knowledge of the track, the electrical equipment, the work that might be taking place "out there" on the infrastructure, and the train service running, as well as their experience of previous similar cases, in order to assess the criticality of the alarm. The strategy at this stage was mostly *similarity matching,* which was highly related to the operators' experience. Usually, this stage was tightly coupled with the analysis and assessment of the alarm.

Information presented to the operator was used for the purpose of assessing and evaluating the underlying meaning and causes of alarms. Operators generally analysed alarms by stretching the existing evidence to match the scenario with similar cases (*extrapolation*). Unlike similarity matching, where all of the evidence was matched with a similar previous alarm, extrapolation requires the operator to use their imagination to fill the gaps until a similarity was found.

The operator identified possible courses of action, evaluated them, and executed the optimum action to clear the alarm. The operator remembered similar cases and tried to match the stretched evidence to other potential (*similarity matching and extrapolation*) causes and trialled the corrective actions of those cases (*trial and error*).

6.5.6 TIMELINE ANALYSIS

Figure 6.4 shows the order and duration of activities when handling unexpected alarm episodes. Unsurprisingly, there was an order to the occurrence of these activities: notification, acceptance, analysis, and clearance. Interestingly, lengthy alarm-handling episodes (e.g., episodes 1, 4, and 10 in Figure 6.5) were triggered by some form of information complexity (i.e., high information in the case of alarm episode 1 and low information in the case of alarm episode 4) and were characterised by longer periods of analysis and clearance. For example, during alarm-handling episode 4, the operator had to investigate a number of possible causes that led to the alarm. Once the operator had identified the type and priority of the alarm and selected the appropriate operational page, they had to explore three possible routes in order to detect the affected circuit breaker that led to the alarm. Upon analysis of the alarm,

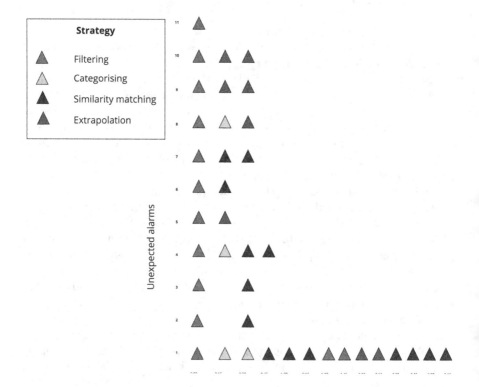

FIGURE 6.5   Order of alarm-handling strategies for unexpected alarms

the operator had to close the circuit breakers one by one to test the resulting impact (the system design did not allow simultaneous closure of the circuit breakers and it took longer than expected to clear the alarm).

Similar mapping activity across the time-stamped observational checklist, and the selected coping strategies, informed the adopted duration of each of the strategies and their order (Figure 6.3). Similar to Figure 6.4, the order of strategies is also consistent. Strategies adopted by the operators and hence supporting/aiding/guiding that particular strategy would assist the operator in a specific phase of the alarm handling (Figure 6.5).

6.6   DISCUSSION

This chapter reports a series of studies that were performed to establish an understanding of alarm handling in ECRs. A combination of qualitative and quantitative methods was adopted to identify operators' activities and strategies while handling alarms.

It was found from operators' comments that strategies such as similarity matching and extrapolation are related to experience and local knowledge. Alarm systems should be designed to provide better support by, for instance, providing historical and statistical information relevant to the alarm. The potential risks are also demonstrated – for example, extrapolation may lead operators to apply inappropriate prior knowledge. Extrapolation is often used as the basis for clearing alarms, albeit with the risk that an inappropriate match could be made between the current case and previous experiences. Therefore, local knowledge and historical information should be available to assist operators in accepting alarms with confidence.

One particular finding of the study is the comparison between expected and unexpected alarms. The alarm banner, the display area, and the menu on the operational display are the three most used artefacts for handling unexpected alarms, while the alarm banner and the telephone are the most utilised artefacts when operators are handling expected alarms. This difference is because in the case of an expected alarm, operators only need to verify and confirm an expected event through either a telephone call from a member of the maintenance team or an updated alarm banner. Having said that, the fact that operators are expecting an alarm (due to ongoing engineering work) does not necessarily mean that the next alarm occurring is known and does not need any diagnosis. ECR operators commented on situations where unexpected alarms occurred and were attributed to ongoing engineering work at the time and in the relevant area. Had they not noticed the difference promptly, the misidentification could have led to major issues such as a major fault remaining uncorrected after the engineering work ceases and the area brought back into operation.

Another important finding of this study relates to the comparison between high and low information alarms. When operators are faced with low information, they use the display area almost twice as much as in cases of high information. However, the overall duration of handling high information alarms is twice as long as low information alarms. This could suggest that operators are a lot better at finding the missing information on the operational display than categorising and filtering the high amount of information presented to them. Another explanation could be that current systems are not very good at categorising and filtering information, which should also be a concern for the design of future alarm displays.

One major surprise from this work was the relatively few instances of alarms that actually took place. Despite the 18 hours of field study, only 22 alarms were generated, and discussion with operators revealed that, particularly during the night shift, this kind of workload was fairly typical. However, ECR alarms and work generally are known to be extremely variable.

This would suggest some broader human factors implications with the ECR operators role, in that at periods of low workload there are probably issues around vigilance (Warm et al., 2008). At the other extreme, managing alarms during peak hours contributed to periods of high workload and increased potential for errors during other time-critical tasks. Extreme peaks of work may come in the transition between running service and the night, as engineering teams ask for isolations for overnight trackwork. This peak comes again with the handback to the operational service the next morning (Golightly and Palacin, 2021; Kaul et al, 2022). This suggests that future human factors work in the ECR environment should continue to develop a deeper understanding of the task demands, technological limitations, and resulting cognitive vulnerabilities in order to improve staff wellbeing, the working environment, and the sustainable performance of the system.

6.7 CHAPTER SUMMARY

The work presented in this chapter indicates the complexities of alarm-handling domains. In the next chapter, we will look at ways to structure this kind of work to build an overview of the socio-technical aspects of condition monitoring work, using cognitive work analysis (CWA).

7 Cognitive Work Analysis to Understand Asset Monitoring and Management

7.1 CHAPTER OVERVIEW

Previous chapters have highlighted the human factors for remote condition monitoring and the behaviours and challenges of using this kind of maintenance and asset monitoring system. As stated in Chapter 3, human factors is a holistic approach. Therefore, our methods need to turn a variety of data sources into a form that designers and evaluators can use when building or deploying remote condition monitoring.

This chapter illustrates the use of one such approach cognitive work analysis. This is applied to the rail electrical control example presented in Chapter 6, which requires an understanding of the cognitive task of how electrical control is carried out, the implications of expanding the area of control, and the subsequent potential increase in the information presented to the operator. The key research questions explored in this chapter are:

1. How to implement CWA as a means to incorporate thorough knowledge about tasks, functions, roles, and strategies into systems development and the system life cycle.
2. Linking CWA stages to the design process phases introduced in ISO 11064-1:2001: Ergonomics design of Control Centres.
3. Discuss some of the considerations around the successful application of CWA.

7.2 STAGES OF COGNITIVE WORK ANALYSIS

When analysing and designing work, it is common to describe or prescribe the tasks people engage in and build around that specification. In practice, such an approach can be limiting. It will fail to take into account the full range of constraints that influence work, including competing motivations, and fail to understand the different ways work can be done (some of which may be more effective than others or which may change due to experience and expertise on the part of the operator). What is required is mapping out all of the characteristics of work to design systems that fully reflect the potential range of constraints that will influence successful performance.

DOI: 10.1201/9781315587288-7

Cognitive work analysis is a conceptual and system-based approach for analysing human information interaction in highly dynamic socio-technical workplaces (Sanderson et al., 1999; Fidel and Pejtersen, 2004). It was initially proposed by Rasmussen et al. (1994) and subsequently modified by Vicente (1999) and Lintern (2009).

As noted in Chapter 4, stages of CWA slightly vary (see Table 4.3). Lintern's model is suggested to allow CWA's application at all points of the system life cycle (from requirements to commissioning) rather than merely informing system design (Sanderson et al., 1999). The phases suggested by Lintern (2009) include:

- Work Domain Analysis

Work domain analysis (WDA) focuses on the work's functional (activity-independent) structure. It consists of an abstraction hierarchy (AH) with five levels: domain purpose, domain values and priorities, domain functions, physical functions, and physical objects. Domain purpose refers to the overall objectives of the system; domain values and priorities refer to the necessary characteristics of the system while achieving its goals. Domain function describes what needs to be conducted within the control domain at an abstract level. In contrast, physical functions describe the physical expression that needs to be performed to facilitate those domain functions. Finally, physical objects are the artefacts and tools used in the control room to enable physical functions (Lintern, 2009). Overall, this analysis facilitates an understanding of the work domain and the contextual constraints that may influence the performance of the work.

- Work Task Analysis/Cognitive Transformation Analysis

Work organisation analysis is used to associate tasks required for the domain functions identified in the AH with the situations in which the work occurs. It is common to associate these situations with physical locations. For example, an analysis of aircraft operation may include on the ground, taxiing and take-off, cruising, and landing.

- Strategy Analysis

Human operators tend to adopt strategies and shortcuts to overcome the limitations imposed by technical systems, including inefficient information presentation. As we saw in Chapters 5 and 6, operators have to focus on a number of key information sources concurrently. Hence, they cannot cope with system anomalies like normal situations and must adopt strategies to manage the alarm. Hollnagel and Woods (2005) listed the strategies potentially applied by operators in joint cognitive systems to cope with any complexity, such as the high information density observed in the ECR.

- Cognitive Processing Analysis

Cognitive processing analysis aims to identify the operator's processing mode while attending to work tasks. This stage provides designers with the information that operators will mainly require based on the cognitive processing modes. Cognitive processing mode is categorised into rule-based, skill-based, and knowledge-based behaviour. Therefore, each task identified in a contextual activity matrix and associated strategies would relate to a cognitive processing mode. Identifying these processing modes can then be used to inform design recommendations.

Together, this set of analytical approaches describes the nature of the work, the equipment and purposes of work, and the cognitive manner in which work can be performed. Importantly, this covers not just the design of one technology but also the whole working environment and therefore how the use of one technology might negatively or positively interact with a task performed with another technology. This is useful to RCM given what we have seen in Chapters 5 and 6 about how more than technology can be used to deal with a task.

7.3 APPROACH

Figure 7.1 presents the approach used. This was based on the data collection conducted in Chapter 6. A work domain analysis, organisation of work, and cognitive

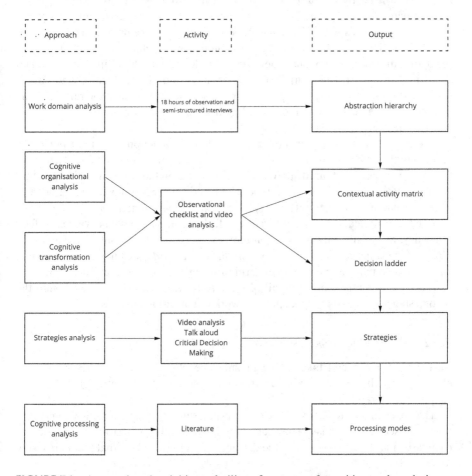

FIGURE 7.1   Approach and activities to facilitate five stages of cognitive work analysis

transformation analysis were developed to provide an initial understanding of the domain. Cognitive strategies and processing modes were also identified to create an understanding of human information processing and some insights into information presentation and formats. Social transaction analysis was not carried out as it was not central to the work being studied.

7.4   ANALYSIS

7.4.1   WORK DOMAIN ANALYSIS

The observational checklist used in Chapter 6 showed the connection between different physical objects and their use for achieving different goals. In addition, operators' comments and talk-aloud sessions highlighted the values and purposes associated with each function.

Figure 7.2 shows an abstraction hierarchy of alarm handling in a rail ECR. Artefacts utilised by operators during alarm handling include SCADA, logbook, phone, map, regulations, and isolation requests. Also, the operator might consult with their colleagues within the control room or call someone on-site to obtain more information. These artefacts enable the operator to understand the system status and the optimum plan he/she ought to develop and follow. Alarm handling can be broken down into two main functions, alarm recognition and alarm clearance, to ensure safety and efficiency for the supply and optimise resources within the railway. This activity is embedded within the overall goal of providing a continuous electricity supply to the rail network.

The AH offers an early understanding of domain functions and their purposes, relating to the "what" and the "why" of alarm handling in a railway ECR. Therefore, this AH gives us a structured approach to understanding the types of constraints that impinge on the operator's work and the relationships between those constraints. For example, one of the constraints is that both of the domain functions (alarm recognition and alarm clearance) are relevant to all domain priorities and values (safety, efficiency, and optimisation). It is common for these values to conflict (Ryan et al., 2021) – for example, it is difficult to maintain safety *and* efficiency. Therefore, any change to a domain function or its underpinning physical function and artefacts must consider the potential impact on all of these priorities. The AH also feeds into the second stage of cognitive work analysis: work organisation analysis.

7.4.2   WORK ORGANISATION ANALYSIS

As the work examined takes place in only one physical location (the ECR), we elected to use the situation axis for different physical systems that might be used to support the work functions.

The boxes in Figure 7.3 show the overall spectrum of the artefacts that can potentially be used for each task. The shaded circles highlight the most used artefact for each task, and the whiskers show the distribution of the artefacts that are more likely to be used.

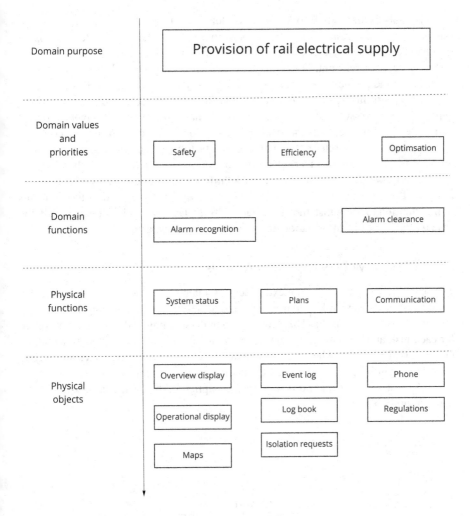

FIGURE 7.2 AH for alarm handling in railway ECRS

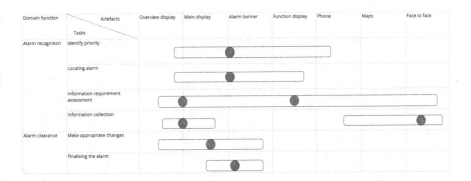

FIGURE 7.3 Alarm handling contextual activity matrix

This analysis allows the work functions identified at the AH stage (alarm recognition and alarm clearance) to be tied to specific work contexts and artefacts. Using the matrix in this way can clarify where each of the constraints identified in the AH may be most relevant. For example, the main display is used in all work tasks. In contrast, the phone is only used in two stages (identify priority and information collection) as in face-to-face communication (information collection and assess the alarm). These two work situations are of particular interest as they involve contact with other human agents in the system, usually for clarification or enhanced information gathering. Therefore, the matrix allows us to represent that, for specific tasks (and not for others), there is a critical role for cooperation in managing the alarm.

Similarly, we can see that the work task "information collection" is relevant to all but one of the work situations. This indicates that the operator needs multiple forms of information to recognise the alarm successfully. However, it is not necessarily the case that all types of information are required for every alarm.

7.4.3 Cognitive Transformation Analysis

The seven tasks noted in the contextual activity matrix were used as the basis for this stage. Operators were asked, retrospectively, to describe the reasoning behind their decisions during these tasks. This provided an understanding of the processes required for each task and the associated states. Operators' comments led to state process diagrams (e.g., Figure 7.4, where curved rectangles represent cognitive states and arrows show the cognitive processes that guide the transitions between cognitive states).

These state process diagrams were then compiled in the form of a decision ladder (e.g., Figure 7.5).

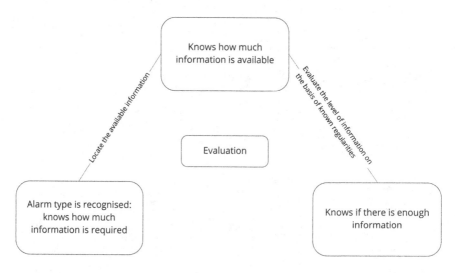

FIGURE 7.4 Example of a state process diagram for the work task of information requirement assessment

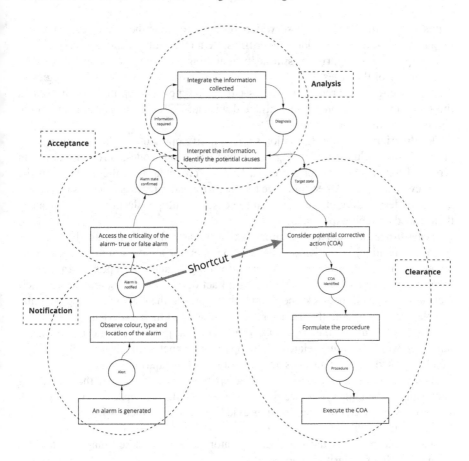

FIGURE 7.5 Alarm handling decision ladder

As discussed in Chapter 5, the decision ladder provides a sequential representation of the cognitive processing relevant to alarm handling. However, it also supports the representation of different routes through the generic process. For example, the bold arrow represents a leap between alarm acceptance and alarm clearance. It reflects the handling of expected maintenance alarms, where the operator has prior knowledge of the likely occurrence of the alarm before the actual generation of that alarm. As a result of this existing prior knowledge, no evaluation or analysis is required. By extension, none of the information sources relevant to evaluation or analysis are therefore required. This also demonstrates the additional steps (and information sources) required when the alarm is genuine (i.e., the additional steps required for alarm acceptance and alarm analysis).

7.4.4 STRATEGY ANALYSIS

In the observations discussed in Chapter 6, participants were prompted to specify which strategy they were using at any given point during alarm cases. This made it possible in the final two observation sessions to infer the strategies from participants' talk-aloud and video recordings. A number of potential strategies (filtering, queuing, categorising, similarity matching, and extrapolation) emerged in the majority of the cases. From this, it was possible to assign specific strategies to high-level cognitive processing stages (strategy types are highlighted in bold in the following discussions), later validated with an ECR operator familiar with the strategy classification.

Notification: several information sources notify operators of the existence of an alarm. These include the flashing alarm banner, colour codes, acronyms of alarm type and location, sirens, phone calls, flashing circles around the location on the overview display, etc. Operators have to categorise and filter these sources to achieve a basic understanding of the alarm. In the case of multiple alarms, operators queue them based on their experience.

Acceptance: the situation awareness that we assume is built into the previous stage (notification) is the basis on which the operator almost immediately accepts the alarm and silences the siren without informing an authorised person. In the rare cases of an alarm where immediate on-site action is required, operators use their local knowledge (of the track, the electrical equipment, the work which might be taking place out there, and the train service running) and their experience of previous similar cases to assess the criticality. The strategy at this stage is mostly similarity matching which is highly related to the operators' experience. Usually, this stage is tightly coupled with the analysis and assessment of the alarm.

Analysis: information presented to the operator is being used by them to assess and evaluate the underlying meaning and causes of alarms. Operators usually analyse alarms by stretching the existing evidence to match them with similar cases (extrapolation). Unlike similarity matching, where all of the evidence is matched with a similar previous alarm and the operator has to use his/her imagination to fill the gaps until a similarity is perceived.

Clearance: the operator identifies possible actions, evaluates them, and executes the optimum action to clear the alarm. The operator remembers similar cases and tries to match the stretched evidence to another potential (similarity matching and extrapolation) causes and trials the corrective actions of those cases (trial and error).

7.4.5 COGNITIVE COMPETENCE ANALYSIS

Figure 7.6 shows the cognitive processing modes associated with various tasks, the artefacts required to conduct those tasks, and an exemplar of design implications to support the corresponding cognitive processing mode. For example, categorising, similarity matching, and filtering are rule-based processing modes when the operator has to apply a set of instructions. The operator has to see the pattern at this level, but that does not necessarily lead to a recognised and clear set of actions. After identifying the pattern, the operator has to set an action plan.

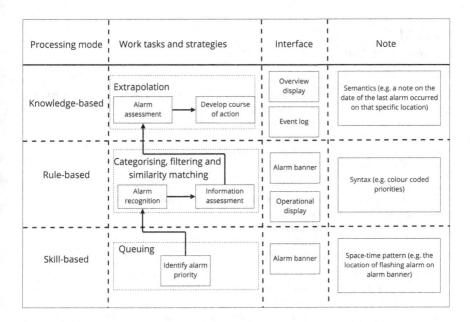

FIGURE 7.6 Cognitive processing modes, alarm activities, and artefacts

7.5 DISCUSSION

This chapter has described the use of five stages of CWA to describe ECR work. What emerges from using these analyses in combination is how the analytical forms work together to build a detailed view of the cognitive requirements of a given work domain. The AH gives us functions embedded in a physical and organisational context. These functions are elaborated in the contextual activity matrix in terms of corresponding tasks and work situations. The cognitive transformations underlying these tasks are represented in the decision ladder, which highlights higher-order stages of processing. These higher-order stages inform strategy analysis and, from this, processing modes which can lead to design requirements.

CWA can then be used to generate specific recommendations. A short list of recommendations emerging from this CWA is presented in Table 7.1.

There are a number of challenges associated with the use of CWA. The effectiveness of a CWA is highly dependent on the availability of data, subject matter experts, and the researcher's expertise in performing the analysis. This may limit the viability of performing all stages within the timescales and resources of a project. To get around this, only a few CWA stages may be carried out, or, as in our case, only certain job functions in a domain are analysed. This chapter has described only one of the functions of ECR operation (alarm handling). It might have proved impossible or of limited use to apply CWA to elaborate every ECR function. The risk is that critical

TABLE 7.1

Example of Findings and Their Application

Recommendations	Rationale	CWA stage	ISO 11064
The information on the alarm banner should be presented in categories, and they should be easily filtered.	Operator's strategies are categorising and filtering the information; therefore, if the information is easily filtered, then it can improve the performance.	Strategy analysis	Concept design
Duplicated sources of information are ignored during notifying the alarm.	The contextual activity matrix showed that during the alarm notification, only the alarm banner was attended.	Work organisation analysis	Analysis and definition
Operators use duplicated information to confirm the existence of the problem and accept the alarm.	The contextual activity matrix as well as the decision ladder confirms that operators attend different information displays before accepting an alarm.	Work organisation analysis and cognitive transformation analysis	Analysis and definition
Provide situational information which is particularly relevant to the situation when operators want to accept the alarm.	Operator's strategies while analysing and clearing the alarm were either to stretch the evidence (extrapolate) or to match the situation with similar situations; therefore, providing situational information that gives the operator a better overview of the problem can be very useful.	Cognitive transformation analysis and strategies analysis	Analysis and definition

interdependencies between people, technology, and functions within the overall system will be lost by focusing on only one aspect of the system. For example, a fuller understanding of how people handle alarms might be gained from the joint analysis of their everyday monitoring, planning, and optimisation activities. Therefore, it may have been valuable to conduct a WDA of the control system as a whole to determine these interdependencies and prioritise the functions that require more analysis.

7.6 CHAPTER SUMMARY

This chapter has described the use of the five stages of CWA in the context of rail ECR operations, particularly handling alarms. The process of data collection, analysis, and interpretation suggests that CWA has value in this case in supporting an understanding of those domain features and subsequent cognitive implications, which can inform design. However, we recommend flexibility in how the stages of CWA are implemented and, indeed, which stages are used so that the study resource expended is proportionate to the value of design life cycle insights gained. Chapter 8 turns from describing current operations to future operations and the human challenges of predictive and intelligent maintenance systems.

8 Defining Intelligent Infrastructure and Identifying the Key Challenges

8.1 CHAPTER OVERVIEW

This chapter presents interviews with key stakeholders (including senior railway managers, operators, and IT specialists) to get their perspectives on the role of human factors in Intelligent Infrastructure. A key deliverable of this work was a data processing framework that is more suited to managing a human factors contribution than the ISO 13774-4:2015 framework. Furthermore, and as we found out through our study, there may be different views on what terminology such as Intelligent Infrastructure might mean and, therefore, an early interview phase can help gauge the perceptions and expectations of an organisation.

This includes understanding the scope of the technology, and the kinds of users and tasks that need to be considered. This work was conducted as interviews with strategists and key managers at the sponsoring organisation – Network Rail – and also with senior managers in the technology supply chain.

The objectives of this chapter are, therefore, to provide:

- A description of the method used to elicit the views of strategists and senior management relevant to the delivery of rail Intelligent Infrastructure
- Identification of key human factors considerations that would affect the successful design and adoption of Intelligent Infrastructure from a user perspective
- Present a framework that maps these user considerations to a more traditional view of remote condition monitoring (i.e., one where data is transformed into information)

It is important to note that the work and analysis were conducted just over 10 years ago. While the general findings still hold and are indeed still coming to light in more recent studies of Intelligent Infrastructure or predictive maintenance in other sectors (e.g., Golightly et al., 2018), we reflect at the end of this chapter on how things progressed.

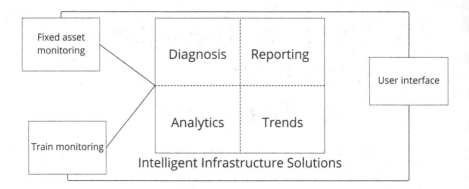

FIGURE 8.1   An overview of RCM in railway

8.2   BACKGROUND

Intelligent Infrastructure systems in Network Rail were initiated in 2006 in response to the need for more reliable service and optimised utilisation of existing infrastructure. Network Rail owns, operates, and develops the Great Britain railway as the infrastructure manager.

The objective of Intelligent Infrastructure, as presented in the good practice guide, is "to deliver improvement by application of intelligence through the infrastructure design and maintenance cycle" (Network Rail et al., 2009). Collecting and analysing integrated information about the condition of railway assets was expected to improve maintenance efficiencies, enhance safety and operational performance, and lead to a more affordable railway.

Network Rail's high-level model of remote condition monitoring is shown in Figure 8.1. This is a very simple workflow; it shows the data sources, transformation links, a strategic Intelligent Infrastructure solution, and end-user interfaces. Little was known at the start of the Intelligent Infrastructure project about the knowledge and information requirements that would enable the "black" box in the middle of the diagram to provide "Intelligent Infrastructure solutions".

This model starts highlighting some of the key features, but very little is noted with regards to how these features need to be explored, and what is required to understand user experiences and system requirements.

ISO 13374-4:2015 was initially used by the project team to facilitate an approach to develop and deliver advanced condition monitoring and diagnostics. The standard also gives initial guidance for the HMI of such systems through developing an understanding of the current state of the assets (health assessment) and estimating future health conditions (prognostic assessment) and consequently generating operation and maintenance advisories (advisory generation). Having said that, the standard tells us what is needed to be achieved rather than a guide regarding how to achieve them. Built around a six-stage process architecture (see Figure 8.2) comprising:

1. Data acquisition
2. Data manipulation

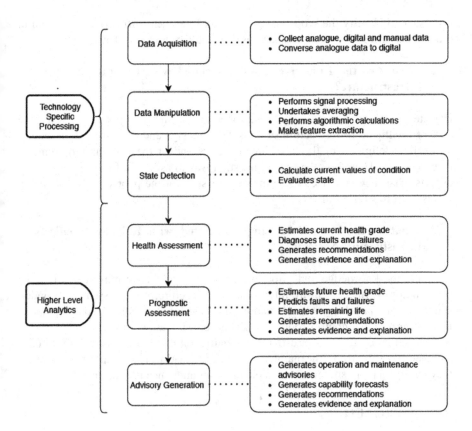

FIGURE 8.2   ISO 13374 strategic framework taken from Network Rail 2009

3. State detection
4. Health assessment
5. Prognostic assessment
6. Advisory generation

Chapter 2 introduced the technical background to RCM and also introduced the key framework ISO 13374. The standard although develops a high-level understanding of the issues and considerations needed for RCM solutions, they need to be understood in their context of use. The implementation of these standards would need to be modified to the specifics of any deployment domain, functions, and roles. Therefore there is a need to develop not just HMI design guidance but also guidance on the wider human factors and more general human-centred deployment of Intelligent Infrastructure technology. This posed three research questions that drove the study presented in this chapter:

1. What Is Railway Intelligent Infrastructure?

At the time of conducting this study (2010), there was no consistent understanding of Intelligent Infrastructure within the GB railway community. It was, therefore, necessary to identify the scope and goals of an Intelligent Infrastructure system in order to determine the functions and roles that would be influenced by its introduction.

2. What Are the Human Factors Associated with Railway Intelligent Infrastructure?

Despite greater levels of automated data collection and analysis, people are still at the core of Intelligent Infrastructure systems. Good design and implementation require an explicit definition of the key human factors and of the systems requirements they generate. Therefore, the second question was to ascertain from subject matter experts what they perceived to be the major issues for the people using Intelligent Infrastructure within rail.

3. What Is the Data Processing Associated with Railway Intelligent Infrastructure Systems?

To guide the knowledge and information required for better implementation and presentation of future railway Intelligent Infrastructure, it was essential to understand the anticipated flow of information and stages of work conducted by operators in existing railway control rooms. A second consideration was whether this flow was the same for all users or differed depending on the user's responsibilities (e.g., whether they were front-line maintenance staff responding to fault alarms or whether they were in a more strategic role in planning maintenance programmes).

8.3   APPROACH

The approach taken to understand the scope of the domain was semi-structured interviews with key stakeholders. These "subject matter experts" would lay out the scope and expectations of Intelligent Infrastructure and highlight issues that would affect the use of Intelligent Infrastructure.

In order to maximise these stakeholder interviews (often with senior management with limited time), it was necessary first to plan the interview. This was achieved by the lead investigator spending time as a participant observer at the lead organisation, Network Rail, and attending workshops where Intelligent Infrastructure was being scoped. This helped to determine:

1. A question guide that would target the most relevant information from each stakeholder.
2. A potential structure for the framework that would support mapping out the key human factors issues. This structure was identified as ISO 13374 (Figure 8.3).

Transcripts were coded three times to explore different perspectives associated with Intelligent Infrastructure. The first round of coding was focused on developing a general understanding of railway Intelligent Infrastructure. Issues associated with

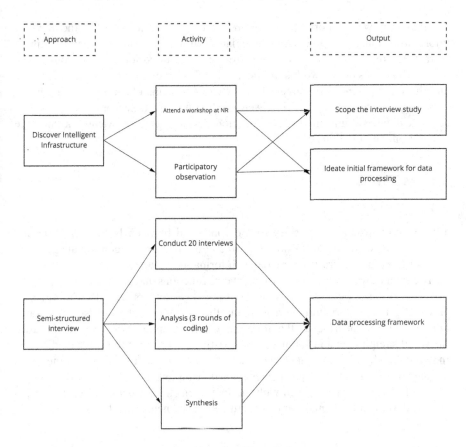

FIGURE 8.3 Approach to explore railway Intelligent Infrastructure

definitions, benefits, roles, and functionalities of railway Intelligent Infrastructure were explored.

The second round of coding addressed human factors issues. It was clear from the general description of Intelligent Infrastructure that although Intelligent Infrastructure itself is a relatively new area for human factors research and guidance, there were a number of human factors contributions which would help our understanding. Examples of such human factors research include the development of insight and guidance for collaborative engineering (Patel et al., 2012), socio-technical systems (Carayon, 2006), and adaptive and human-centred automation (Kaber and Endsley, 2004), to name a few. In addition, one of the questions asked was focused on the potential challenges of the project, mainly to encourage participants to talk about different problems specifically focused on development and implementation. These challenges then corresponded to potential human factors considerations, such as mental models, decision-making, monitoring, organisational culture, planning, human reliability, situation awareness, user engagement, and workload. The interpretation was further confirmed with another human factors expert to ensure reliability.

Finally, it was important to capture participants' views about the flow of information and data processing associated with the future railway Intelligent Infrastructure. The transcripts were therefore re-reviewed for the third round, this time with a focus on the work and information flow of current RCM systems in use and those for potential Intelligent Infrastructure systems of the future. The headings used to organise this review were as follows: asset, sensor, data, data processing, database, information, information development, knowledge, knowledge integration, and intelligence.

8.4 METHOD

8.4.1 PARTICIPANTS

Twenty semi-structured interviews were conducted between November 2009 and January 2010 with rail staff knowledgeable about or were potential managers and users of Intelligent Infrastructure and its information systems.

The interviewees were drawn from several functions and levels of seniority. The first interviewees were chosen based on the suggestions of experts who attended an Intelligent Infrastructure workshop and the recommendation of Network Rail's Director of Engineering at the time; snowball sampling was used afterwards. Snowball sampling is a technique to ask existing participants to introduce different individuals who are associated with the project. They will be asked to introduce another round of potential participants. Participants were drawn from the companies and organisations involved with the Intelligent Infrastructure project – supply chains, developers, and major infrastructure enhancement projects.

8.4.2 DESIGN

Information sheets were sent to participants before the study to introduce the research aims and to provide a set of questions to be asked during the study. These questions (formed during the familiarisation process and were confirmed by Network Rail's Director of Engineering at the time) were:

1. What do you understand to be the future of Intelligent Infrastructure for Network Rail?
2. What do you think is the purpose of Intelligent Infrastructure?
3. Do you consider remote condition monitoring (RCM) as a type of Intelligent Infrastructure?
4. What does "remote" in RCM mean?
5. What does "intelligent" in Intelligent Infrastructure mean?
6. How will the information required for an Intelligent Infrastructure be captured?
7. What do you think are the main functions of an Intelligent Infrastructure information display?

8. Which control rooms need to be in direct contact with Intelligent Infrastructure systems?
9. What are the challenges in designing an effective Intelligent Infrastructure system?
10. What are the main roles and responsibilities of operators working with Intelligent Infrastructure systems?

However, the structure was applied in quite an informal manner. Participants were encouraged to comment on topics associated with Intelligent Infrastructure beyond what was asked; depending on their expertise and domain of work, some questions were elaborated, whereas some remained unexplored. All interviews were audio recorded with the participants' consent as this allowed the interviewer to focus on the discussion and for the interviews to be fully transcribed afterwards.

8.4.3 ANALYSIS

Twenty hours of interviews were transcribed (approximately 55,000 words) and analysed. Thematic content analysis (Miles and Huberman, 1994; Neale and Nichols, 2001) followed by an inter-rater reliability analysis of selected interviews.

All of the themes used in the three rounds of coding were commented on by two members of Network Rail's Ergonomics team. Furthermore, to facilitate the assessment of the consistency of the coding, one of the members of the Ergonomics team coded two of the interviews and offered comments on how the coding approach was used.

8.5   FINDINGS

This section summarises the findings from the interview studies to inform the three perspectives and help explore the following questions:

1. What is Intelligent Infrastructure?
2. What are applicable human factors issues associated with Intelligent Infrastructure?
3. What is the flow of information within future Intelligent Infrastructure?

8.5.1   RAILWAY INTELLIGENT INFRASTRUCTURE

Intelligent Infrastructure in Network Rail has been defined pragmatically as a means of support to enable more reliable and effective railway maintenance. However, the extent of its capabilities varies in the eyes of different potential users. Although individual interviewees did not have a consistent definition of the concept, the data collected from the sample did help with an understanding of the potential functionalities, roles, benefits, and human factors involved in railway Intelligent Infrastructure. Maintenance staff (maintenance control centre, railway engineering) viewed the systems as somewhat more advanced RCM systems, members of the infrastructure investment and corporate development teams viewed it as pioneering technology that could "solve all" railway problems, while others were more cautious:

> We need to diagnose from the data we have and inform the relevant people, otherwise, that data is pointless.

The consensus of the interviews was that Intelligent Infrastructure provides information about assets to support real-time condition monitoring and high-level asset management. Potential benefits of Intelligent Infrastructure are targeted at safety and efficiency more informed and effective maintenance regime. Interviewees noted that the intelligence could either be built into the asset or can lie in the interpretation of the information captured from that asset, thus supporting diagnosis, prediction, or initiation of repair or replacement.

The distribution of Intelligent Infrastructure can be layered and can happen both centrally and locally, meaning that there is a multiplicity of human and computer roles and responsibilities with different demands and priorities. Three main human roles for the first wave of implementations were identified in the interviews as control room operators, track workers, and strategic analysts.

Control room operators are responsible for responding instantly to high-priority alarms. They are based in local or regional control rooms, supporting an operational railway by interpreting alerts and other information, making diagnoses, and planning for corrective actions, such as repairs or replacement. Track workers receive information from control room operators regarding a potential failure and then feedback information about the condition of that asset obtained from onsite visits. Staff in control rooms (and/or possibly on track) will be informed of a defect through an alarm or an alert; their knowledge of the environment (showing the importance of "local knowledge"), their understanding of the asset criticality, and of the level of risk associated with that fault will support the choice of corrective actions. The control room operators need different engineering know-how to interpret the traces and graphs. Different assets (e.g., catch pits, embankments, S&C, plain line track, etc.) all fail differently and require diverse domain expertise to diagnose and skills to fix. The level of risk also depends on timing factors and location. Strategic analysts receive diagnostic reports from control room operators to make decisions about plans, speed restrictions, maintenance regimes, etc., before feeding that information back to control room operators and track workers. Within future Intelligent Infrastructure, this higher-level analysis is conducted in central control locations, where responsibilities lie for informing future policy and strategy towards adjustments, metrics, trends, and other parameters to support permanent corrective actions. The view was that it is highly likely that with increased use of advanced Intelligent Infrastructure, these roles will possibly merge, with track staff being responsible for more responses to alarms or control room operators triggering onsite robotic repair devices or improvements in future systems, e.g., tribological design considerations. The main functions of all staff interacting with railway Intelligent Infrastructure systems will be monitoring, problem-solving, alarm handling, fault finding, diagnosis, planning, and optimisation. The human–machine interfaces must support not just one but all of these functions.

Interviewees' knowledge of existing RCM systems, and their assumptions about the proposed Intelligent Infrastructure system, led to the identification of a number of challenges. Technical challenges were mainly noted by the members of the Information Management team, who are responsible for designing and managing the development of the pilot Intelligent Infrastructure system. Examples of these challenges include collecting and monitoring asset data (e.g., trains) to have more accurate Global Positioning Systems (GPS) and algorithms for predictive intelligence. These challenges were reported as manageable, but business change or corporate development challenges could have a fundamental impact. These raise human factors problems such as user engagement, users with different priorities (e.g., the day-to-day realities of the overarching strategic conflict between running trains and carrying out engineering work), enabling diagnosis to optimise performance without risking safety, and undertaking safety-critical assurance.

8.5.2 HUMAN FACTORS

The second round of coding analysed the interview transcriptions in terms of the human factors associated with the potential Intelligent Infrastructure systems as they were perceived at the time of the interviews. These are presented as counts in Figure 8.4 with details in Table 8.1.

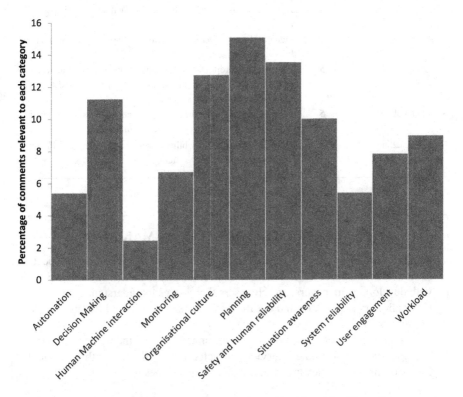

FIGURE 8.4 Interview analysis: human factors issues in railway Intelligent Infrastructure

TABLE 8.1
Human Factors Issues Identified from the Interview Study

Human factors issues	%	Relevance to the Intelligent Infrastructure
Planning	15	Planning can refer to a wide range of activities and policies from strategic allocation of Intelligent Infrastructure roles, maintenance resources, and planning a job to plan the most optimal course of action so that it keeps the balance between safety and operation of the service.
Safety and human reliability	14	To understand potential sources of error and to mitigate the risks associated with them.
Organisational culture	13	To involve various roles and different attitudes towards technical advancements, role changes, business changes, etc.
Decision-making	11	To understand the processes involved with current and future railway decision-making, ultimately to inform optimal decision aids.
Situation awareness	10	To determine knowledge in the head and knowledge in the world regarding system status, operability, and behaviour that is or will be required by the railway operators.
Workload	9	To determine the effects of the introduction of the new technology as well as concomitant changes to maintenance processes, job design, and information and data flows on the current workload.
User engagement	8	To engage end users with the project and facilitate a participatory design approach.
Monitoring	7	To identify issues affecting the performance of monitoring and how this will be changed.
Automation	5	To determine appropriate levels of automation that are practical to the nature of the roles, including allocation of function, data design, and adaptive automation strategies.
System reliability	5	To design and develop reliable systems and issues associated with users' reliance on, and trust in, the systems.
Human–machine interface	3	To identify and address usability issues in order to design effective, efficient, and satisfactory systems.

A SCENARIO IN RAIL DECISION-MAKING

Scenarios are often a useful way of communicating the issues or design aspects of how technology is used. These textual descriptions can then be discussed with developers, managers, and the users themselves to understand how much they reflect current work and future work or how they could be adapted to improve work.

A scenario proved a useful way of summarising how the different human factors issues found in the interviews affected potential work with Intelligent Infrastructure with relevant human factors in parentheses.

Scenario: A circuit breaker is located in a very busy junction (*local knowledge*); it has two other circuit breakers adjacent to it (*situation awareness*). Sensors attached to the circuit breaker record information about its condition every 30 seconds (*system reliability*) and send them to a database (*system reliability*). The data stored will be analysed through pre-defined algorithms to enable state detection (*automation*). If it has a significantly different condition from the circuit breakers' normal condition, it will generate an alarm (*automation*) to inform the operator about the abnormality (*monitoring*). The operator receives the alarm and analyses it to find the potential causes of the detected abnormality (*decision-making*). He/she uses the information presented on the SCADA (Supervisory Control and Data Acquisition) systems (*human–machine interaction, monitoring, automation, system reliability*) and consults with his/her colleagues (*organisational culture, collaboration*) to diagnose the fault (*decision-making*) and to plan for the potential corrective action required. Following this understanding, the operator has to plan (*planning*) the optimum corrective action (*safety and human reliability*) and to do so he/she has to consider external factors (*situation awareness*) such as time of failure (e.g., peak time) and the feasibility of track access to conduct onsite maintenance work.

This scenario shows that in most cases several human factors codes were included in the analysis, emphasising the interdependencies and complexities in Intelligent Infrastructure. Also, some of the factors (e.g. systems reliability) are tangentially associated with human factors, especially when the system is viewed as the human–machine, or socio-technical, and not purely the technical system. Although they mostly had a technical orientation, participants highlighted the need to understand the role of the human operator, and its effect on workload, task design, situation awareness, decision-making, monitoring, human–computer interaction, planning, system reliability, and organisational culture and the fundamental need for systems thinking to explore socio-technical systems.

Participants noted that one of the key challenges facing Intelligent Infrastructure lies around planning. Introducing new technology that aims to centralise and integrate existing technologies will affect how people perceive and perform their roles. This is mainly because new methods of diagnosis and prognosis will be adopted, meaning that experienced operators will have to depart from their traditional ways of working. Intelligent Infrastructure is viewed as a decision aid; participants (mainly at the managerial level) viewed Intelligent Infrastructure as beneficial since it can analyse many parameters simultaneously and would lead to "better" decisions. However, technicians and operators stated concerns about being out of the loop.

There are huge amounts of expertise involved with the decision-making and fault finding, a lot of people (designers and developers) are being surprised by knowing what exactly happens to an asset. To be honest, we really want to know how an expert does their job.

Introducing prognostics functionality, and being able to predict an asset's life, requires a detailed situational understanding. Therefore, situation awareness should be supported by the Intelligent Infrastructure socio-technical system and the interface. In addition, from a process point of view, different operators with various roles and responsibilities, and priorities would utilise Intelligent Infrastructure. Understanding the context of their work setting and their requirement during various stages of their activities is essential.

Participants have identified Intelligent Infrastructure as ideally a self-monitoring and self-diagnosis interface, but experience shows that people have to react as supervisory controllers.

They will have to monitor and merge a combination of remote condition monitoring data, prediction, and decisions emerging from Intelligent Infrastructure and, for some, the traditional information from visual inspection.

Handling faults within a rail environment requires planning between various control centres and operators. For example, the maintenance team should be informed about safe access to the tracks by the electrical controllers. Signallers should know the implication of failures in their area and their impact on their adjacent control sectors. All of these activities require planning and an overall understanding of railway operations. Furthermore, even though this is the current picture, in the future, it should not be like this; Intelligent Infrastructure can act as an enabler for organisational change to improve overall maintenance strategy. Successful implementation means understanding the impact of changes on the overall organisation:

> I think the biggest challenges are with people and culture, information management may provide the system that would tick the boxes, but unless we actually get their understanding on board as early as possible then you are doing nothing.

This includes the need to understand the effect on various roles and how to engage the broader organisation with the project to facilitate system acceptability.

Looking through the findings from the interview study and in relation to the data processing framework of the discussion, it appeared that human factors could be clustered into three high-level groups corresponding to different roles and activities. Task design, workload, and human–computer interaction relate to the need for successful manipulation of raw data into meaningful information, presented efficiently and without imposing an unmanageable workload. Monitoring, decision-making, and problem-solving relate to diagnostic roles where operators apply their expertise to understand and manage a fault. Finally, planning and organisational culture should be in place to ensure that the system works as a whole and it is beneficial for the larger railway operation.

8.5.3 Data Processing in Railway Intelligent Infrastructure Systems

The third round of coding focused on the flow of data and informed a data processing framework. The terms/themes explored as part of this third round of coding are used here to emphasise the data transformation and how it will evolve from raw data collected from an asset to an intelligent and optimised decision. As one of the interviewees noted:

> Intelligence is when we are able to use data to prevent equipment failures. So going back to the ISO standard in these six steps, the level of intelligence is increasing. The infrastructure has no level of intelligence in it. (Figure 8.5)

The following describes the different features of data processing and the data processing framework to be shown below.

Asset: any feature used to facilitate the running of the railway – a wide range of equipment on track, such as rails, point machines, level crossings, signals, and the embankments where the rail tracks are located – are assets. Control room equipment such as signalling systems or electrical control room SCADA systems is also considered railway assets.

Sensor: assets are remotely located and spread over a very large area with sensors used to enable the collection of data. Sensors range from RCM equipment attached

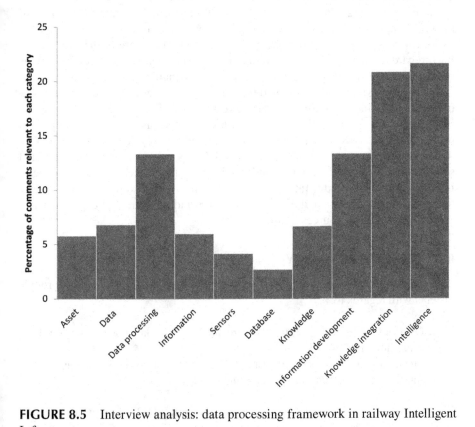

FIGURE 8.5 Interview analysis: data processing framework in railway Intelligent Infrastructure

to the point machines to event frequency collectors at ticket barriers to count the number of passengers on each train.

Data: every asset has a number of attributes, such as age, type, location, etc. Assets also have associated dynamic attributes, such as the current voltage in a point machine or the temperature. Data are logged and collected through sensors and then stored.

Database: the data collected are stored in large databases that can be relational or distributed.[1]

Information: the data in the database have to be interpreted to become meaningful. Attributes, such as the temperature of a point heater, would be analysed based on known standards, with values, discrepancies, and trends available to operators, using simple Excel spreadsheets or much more sophisticated information displays.[2]

Information development: being presented with a piece of information would not lead to action. The agent (human operator or computer) should analyse and assess the available information and develop an understanding of the situation.

Knowledge: information is developed into knowledge through the use of advanced diagnostic, predictive, or reasoning technologies (i.e., machine learning and artificial intelligence) or human expertise to extend the understanding of the situation.

Knowledge integration: the railway is a multi-agent and distributed system, and in order to assess a situation optimally, it is necessary to integrate knowledge from various work settings. For example, a signaller should be aware of the situation on track regarding how protection is set up and the work that is being carried out, as well as train movements planned from an adjacent signalling control centre.

Intelligence: knowledge integrated from different sources is synthesised and contributes to selecting appropriate and effective actions. This intelligence relates to any supporting decision aid, a planning tool, or a knowledge base. At present, only people can make such decisions, but intelligence will eventually be built into an asset.

The interviewees were least concerned with issues associated with databases and sensors, mainly because of their confidence in the available technological advances. Intelligence and knowledge integration received the highest expressions of concern, reflecting the importance and difficulty of understanding operators' expertise when dealing with multiple sources of information.

8.6   CHAPTER SUMMARY

This chapter has presented a qualitative interview study. The key findings provide insights with regards to:

1. Overview of Intelligent Infrastructure, its definition, key obstacles, and relevant human factors issues
2. Phases of development, corresponding design components in line with Intelligent Infrastructure, and alignment to ISO 13374

The outputs of the interviews have been compared with ISO13374 to give us a picture of how different human factors, concerns, and needs are applied across the levels of the architecture. Most importantly, this demonstrates that defining processes and needs at information and intelligence levels is as vital as having clear requirements at the data level. Inspection of the outputs from the three different coding iterations (Intelligent Infrastructure, human factors, and data processing) lead to the development of the framework presented in Chapter 9.

NOTES

1. This is now focused on cloud infrastructure and cloud compute– not the case when the study was done, but it is now a key component and consideration that should/can change the nature of the work.
2. There are no spreadsheets now. These are online dashboards that update in real time.

9 Final Remarks

9.1 CHAPTER OVERVIEW

The previous chapters of this book have introduced the importance of exploring the context of use, cognitive activities conducted by users, and their requirements when designing and developing remote condition monitoring. We have presented studies to showcase how to explore users and direct this in-depth understanding towards better socio-technical systems. In other words, exploring what is intelligent in the workplace can and should guide the data collection and presentation (not the other way around). This chapter presents the book's key contributions and provides high-level guidance for developing user-centred RCM in terms of design guidance and methods.

In doing so, this chapter includes:

- Overview of the key findings
- Presenting a model to understand how people and RCM interact, particularly to deliver advanced prognostics
- A general summary of the implications, with a demonstration of how they apply to another domain
- Closing comments

9.2 OVERVIEW OF KEY FINDINGS

Initially, we identified that RCM, and associated technologies, such as e-maintenance or predictive maintenance, is a significant trend for managing infrastructure and technical assets. Technological advancements such as IoT and distributed systems enable this trend, and the exponential dependence on digitalisation in recent years will accelerate this trend even more. While we focus on rail infrastructure in this book as our case study, it is just as relevant to highways, water, power infrastructure, process control sectors, service design, and the monitoring and managing of a whole range of domestic and industrial products.

We have also outlined that while technology is advancing at great speed, there is some evidence in the research literature and growing anecdotal evidence of solutions that fail to live up to expectations or where their potential is underutilised. This is often due to a range of potential human factors issues, which we present in Chapter 3 of this book. What is required is an approach that explores human performance and real, contextualised decision-making, to understand how tools and technologies can be best applied to support an effective digital experience.

This book presented a series of studies using rail infrastructure as the case study domain, examining the needs and delivery of information and knowledge

TABLE 9.1

Overview of Studies and Key Findings Presented in This Book

Chapter	Summary of the studies reported	Key findings
5	Review of railway maintenance control	• Understanding key activities associated with railway maintenance • Explore resources available *for* maintenance control • Review cognitive aspects of fault finding within maintenance control • Explore cognitive system engineering methods (Critical Decision Method) to understand the complexity of socio-technical systems
6	Review of railway electrical control	• Understand the context associated with railway electrical control rail ECR alarm handling • Explore resources and artefacts available to operators • Review alarm-handling processes, obstacles, and strategies adopted by operators
7	Cognitive work analysis of alarm handling in railway electrical control	• Conduct five stages of cognitive work analysis • Develop an understanding of cognitive aspects associated with alarm handling • Develop an understanding of the methods and their feasibility and practicality
8	Explore railway Intelligent Infrastructure	• Develop an understanding of Intelligent Infrastructure with the railway • Explore relevant human factors issues • Review activities and information processing associated with future railway Intelligent Infrastructure

management for remote condition monitoring systems from a human factors viewpoint. The key findings of this work enabled an in-depth understanding of alarm handling and fault finding as key functions of future remote condition monitoring systems and indicative of some of the relevant human supervisory control functions. The results of studies 1–4 (Chapters 5–8) are summarised in Table 9.1.

One of the key outcomes of this work has been to develop a data processing framework, which reflects the needs of human decision-making. We discuss this framework, next.

9.2.1 Data Processing Framework

Studies in Chapters 5–7 shed light on the types of information processing and decision-making that occur in RCM. Furthermore, the output of the interviews in Chapter 8 led to a synthesised framework, presented in Figure 9.1.

Guidance	Associated cognitive stages + strategies	Rationale
Reduce the number of alarms and faults	Notification and acceptance Filtering and categorising	A large number of alarms were logged, many of which were false and nuisance alarms, and occasionally, they were misleading and caused the operator to miss the real alarms. Intelligent screening and sorting will be required (although the history of alarm mismanagement from human factors literature shows that this is easier said than done).
Integrate the remote condition monitoring and fault management system	Analysis Similarity matching Extrapolation	There are various forms of remote condition monitoring and fault management systems available to the operators. This problem is twofold: on the one hand, the future maintenance control centres have to collate probably inconsistent data to generate consistent advice to the operators. On the other hand, operators can get confused if their systems are showing them repetitive data in different forms and types.
Avoid presenting too much information to the operators	Acceptance and analysis Similarity matching Extrapolation and frequency gambling	Most coping strategies recorded during the CDM interviews refer to those targeted at coping with too much information. It is important to identify and apply sufficient information to the operators. Moreover, transferring a huge amount of data from sensors and loggers to information displays in a control room can be very costly.
Provide a reminder facility on the interface	Analysis and clearance Filtering and categorising	Operators used paper-based reminders to make sure they would attend to the important faults. It is important to assess the optimal format of the reminder facility (i.e., on paper).
Provide information in a way that is easily categorised	Notification and acceptance Categorising and filtering	Fault-finding strategies when operators notice and accept faults are generally through categorising and filtering the data. MCC operators categorise and filer alarm banners and capture the cues associated with identifying and handling specific fault episodes. Designers and developers can support this strategy by providing data in a more distinct format that is easier to categorise.

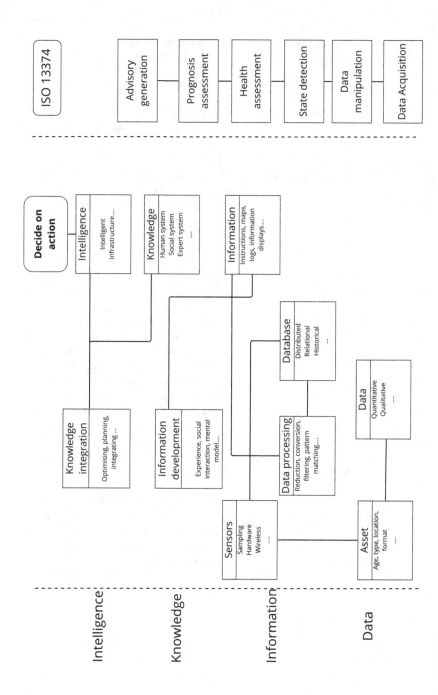

FIGURE 9.1 Data processing framework of railway Intelligent Infrastructure

Four levels of understanding have been specified:

1. Data: facts, not yet interpreted
2. Information: relationships between, and integration of, the facts, maybe in the form of cause and effect relationships
3. Knowledge: interpretation and reasoning applied to the information
4. Intelligence: consideration of the asset, its condition, and any problems within the whole socio-technical system to deliver a plan of action

The framework shows the transition from raw data captured from an asset to a database that keeps all recorded data and the processes required to interpret these (e.g., algorithms, thresholds), leading to a "smart" course of action.

In addition, we aligned the framework with ISO 13374 so that system engineers familiar with ISO 13374 can relate. Data and information layers correspond to stages 1, 2, and 3 of ISO 13374 and enable remote condition measurement of the infrastructure by capturing, sensing, recording, and processing the raw data. The knowledge layer corresponds to the fourth stage of ISO 13374 and enables RCM via the development of the information. Finally, the intelligence layer corresponds to stages 5 and 6 of ISO 13374 and allows remote condition management by integrating the knowledge within various external effectors.

Working at the different horizontal levels within the framework – data, information, knowledge, and intelligence – can guide development teams (including ergonomists) in developing user and human factors requirements, appropriate implementation of automation, job design, teamwork, communications, and procedures.

The tasks associated with data and information can include a rule-based collection and storage of the measured data in a distributed database and are typically straightforward to embed as automated processing. The key factor that designers should consider is ensuring the reliability of the data. This shapes the workload of those to whom Intelligent Infrastructure data are supplied and their trust in the information provided. Designers also need to consider the optimum forms of on-screen information presentation and whether information needs to be "pushed" as alarms or "pulled" (browsed or searched).

Not surprisingly, the other two levels, knowledge and intelligence, which involve more significant information integration, problem-solving, and prediction, are more challenging to automate. It might be possible to introduce semi-automated decision support systems at local levels (e.g., weather monitoring systems in maintenance control centres). However, for a centralised system such as Intelligent Infrastructure, a key benefit lies in the integration of information and knowledge collected from a number of control centres across the country (or at least the performance and contingency plans in the adjacent control rooms to assist the controller in planning optimal courses of corrective action).

Therefore, it is essential to understand how operators attempt to solve their problems. To make sensible decisions about the types and levels of data processing and related operations systems, thorough background knowledge is required about the

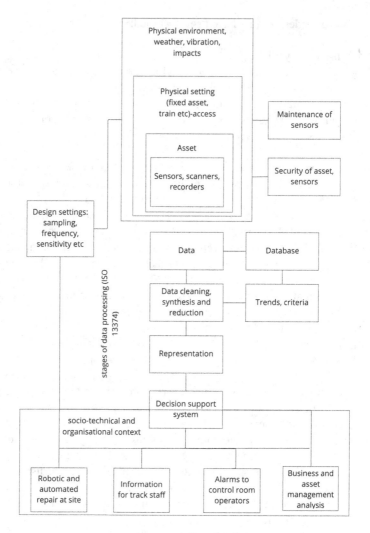

FIGURE 9.2   Wider systems representation of Intelligent Infrastructure

existing functions and roles of the potential major user groups. This was covered for control room operators in the studies presented in Chapters 5–7.

Also, based on the interviews reported in Chapter 8, while senior managers can offer us an excellent overview of the intentions of Intelligent Infrastructure, they seemed to be limited in their understanding of what happens on the ground – this is sometimes described as the difference between "Work as Imagined" vs. "Work as Done". This also means that observing actual operators in situ is essential to validate our findings from the interview. So, in other words, to capture the "intelligence", it is vital to move beyond reviewing procedures and manuals. It is essential to explore what is "work as done". This not only creates a real-world understanding of the context but also allows for identifying motivations and priorities and consequently informs the designing of user interfaces that are more likely to be accepted by their specific user groups.

One of the earliest mantras behind the moves to Intelligent Infrastructure is the desire to move from a find-and-fix philosophy and approach to one of predict and prevent. This raises interesting questions for the system's planners and designers of where exactly and by what/who the prediction and prevention will be carried through. With find and fix, there was no doubt – finding faults was through staff out on the track or by operators interpreting alarms and alerts in control centres, with the fix being largely carried out by teams of specialist staff on site. The big question, then, is how our developed framework will support role allocation and work bank decisions within the Intelligent Infrastructure system. For the wider socio-technical systems concerns and requirements to be better understood, the schematic shown in Figure 9.2 has been produced.

It is through knowledge of the goals and functions of the different roles involved in making future Intelligent Infrastructure a success and the capabilities of those filling the roles (including elements of automated and robotic systems) that socio-technical design decisions will be made. Many of the key functions which are removed from the immediate interaction with Intelligent Infrastructure will involve planning and decision-making – for instance, decisions on sensitivity settings and sampling rates for sensors, data cleaning, and reduction/representation, and on the use of on-track staff, control room operators, or robotics repair to implement the preventive mechanisms. What will underpin many of the organisational and technical systems design decisions will be how managers and engineers view the system. Suppose a narrow technological focus is taken, with the system being the hardware and software. In that case, the organisation of maintenance and renewal work will be very different than if a socio-technical systems view dominates, whereby decisions over what work is to be done and when are made by a joint human–machine system.

9.2.2 Implications for Design and Deployment

The fundamental implication of the framework presented in Figure 9.1 is that too often the RCM technology is designed based on the data, with the transition to decision-making and intelligence treated as something of an afterthought. Often the data is collected in response to a specific infrastructure risk, or sometimes simply because new forms of potentially useful data are available. But unless the data, and algorithms that process the data, are tuned to operational needs, the value is lost.

The work presented in this book suggests tuning to operational needs requires thought at two levels:

1. Within any specific RCM tool – the presentation and processing of data must be designed to reflect the specific decision-making needs of an individual. This is more than just data presentation and visualisation (though that is crucial). We often found that users needed to navigate through sets of data and therefore their ability to control the movement through

information – to search, browse, interrogate, and group information – is vital to it for performing problem-solving and therefore valuable work. Many of the operators we observed were time pressured and therefore had to resort to coping strategies, which would impede or bias data processing if not executed carefully. However, we also observed instances where people were more involved in problem-solving – this was often to detect if a fault was genuine and diagnose a fault. Alarms and alerts are critical, but designing for user "pull" of information is also important, particularly for more strategic or planning roles.

2. Within the wider work context – it is common (in *any* ICT project) for designers and developers to focus on their own technology and to oversimplify the work context. In practice, RCM tools will often be just one of many tools in the working environment. More often than not, the well-crafted RCM tool will end up being one tab in a browser on one of six or eight monitors on a desk. Not only does the display of information and language need to be consistent with other tools, but the workflow also needs to consider how a user may use a suite of tools in combination to diagnose and decide on a course of action. While any one technology may not deliver the full transition from data to intelligence, *the combination of a number of tools plus the user's own experience and problem-solving will provide that intelligence* – this is the essence of a joint cognitive system (Hollnagel and Woods, 2005). New technologies must be procured, designed, and deployed in that light. Tools like contextual observation (Chapters 5 and 6) and cognitive work analysis (Chapter 7) are critical to helping us see the bigger picture of how technologies will be used.

9.3   APPLICATION AND FUTURE

We have described a framework that reflects the data processing when complex decisions are made. Traditional engineering practice looks at what technology and data are available and then uses this data to inform an effective decision. We argued that this approach is limiting. The approach explored and presented in this book invites designers, developers, and planners to start with understanding intelligence, allowing for selecting relevant and sufficient data. This can be applied to any complex socio-technical system, which in our digitised world is almost every system.

While we have looked at rail, we can consider a different example – that of condition monitoring for wind turbines. Wind turbines placed out at sea are difficult to access and expensive to maintain. There may be many 10s, or even 100s, of turbines in an offshore wind farm. Key parts of each asset include the turbine blades, gearings, and transmission systems that transmit the rotational force of the turbine into a generator, the generator itself, and also the infrastructure (condition of the pilings and shaft) that support the turbine.

At the highest level, we can reflect on the framework in Figure 9.1 and how that might affect the design and deployment of a sensing system, for example, to monitor the condition of gear attached to the turbine. One could design that system by capturing as much data as possible, analysing it, and presenting it to a user, but we would argue that it is as important to work with potential users to understand what technologies and processes they already engage in. This is both to understand the context where new technology is going to be deployed (for the point of consistency of information, for integration within the workplace) and to understand how the technologies they are currently using might be impeding their problem-solving and decision-making. In particular, an analysis of the strategies that users engage with (similar to Chapters 5 and 6) can shed light on where current technologies may be providing too little or too much information. This gives clues for how best to design the new RCM system. For example, with an existing gearing condition monitoring system, it may generate too many spurious alarms because of the way thresholds are set, or may generate presentations of data that require cross-referencing with other information sources, increasing the chance of error. How can a new gear RCM reduce or remove these problems?

Also, taking the approach in Figure 9.1 can shed light on realistic expectations of what the technology will achieve. Designers might aim, or at least hope, to deliver a system that delivers "intelligence", but by understanding the new RCM system in the light of this framework, one can see where the limits of the technology really end. Is it at the information stage? The information development stage? The knowledge stage? By doing this, we can fully understand where operators will need to engage in cognitive activity, together with the technology, to derive plans of intelligent action for maintenance operations. For example, a turbine gear RCM may be able to take data and process it to the level that it delivers a reliable health assessment, but this means it will be a human operator who needs to turn that assessment into a judgement about whether the turbine gear needs to be maintained.

We can use the decision ladder (Chapters 5 and 7) to help us understand this process. How far will the new technology get us from initial data input to the final decision? At which point will the technology need to be augmented by the knowledge and skills of the operator by referring to other technologies or communicating and cooperating with other people (e.g., staff on site carrying out the inspection; managers and supervisors to confirm courses of action). And, as we have seen a number of times in this book, this will change depending on whether the operator has a tactical role ensuring the real-time continuity of the turbine or a more strategic role deciding (for example) when a whole programme of maintenance should take place for an entire wind farm.

And consider again that this RCM system might be one of a suite of tools. For example, it might only be by comparing the predicted time to failure of the gearbox *in combination with* the predicted lifespan of some other monitored component (e.g., the shaft between turbine blades and gearbox) that the operator can make a decision around the best timing to send a maintenance operator out to the wind farm to conduct cost-effective inspection and repair. Therefore, the gear RCM should be designed in a way (similar navigation, similar terms, and similar language) that allows these combined assessments across multiple RCM systems.

9.4   FINAL COMMENTS

The work presented in this book first started over a decade ago, with the preparation of the book beginning around 2020. A key question when preparing the book was whether some of the observations and findings were still relevant. As we continue to work in remote condition monitoring, predictive maintenance, and intelligent systems for asset monitoring and management, we find that the lessons we have learned have become more, not less relevant.

The huge potential to apply cheap sensors to any asset and delivery it rapidly (further enabled recently by the realisation of high-capacity 5G data networks) means that the ability to generate and send data has grown exponentially. Furthermore, since starting the book, we realise we live in an ever more complex and fragile world, so our sensitivity to risk has never been greater. Finally, and particularly during and in the immediate aftermath of COVID, organisations are trying to streamline costs, to centralise and reduce operational overheads.

Therefore, we have three growing pressures on the individual at the end of any RCM system – greater data, increased risk sensitivity, but static (or possibly reduced) resources (see Figure 9.3). Therefore, we find that the themes and methods discussed in this book are more relevant than ever, and the need to design with the operator in mind is never more valuable.

As we go forward, our work is getting us to think about user-centred RCM in new contexts – rail rolling stock, physical and geotechnical structures for managing risks such as landslips, understanding the risk of extreme weather, and understanding monitoring for new transport modes such as shared e-scooter schemes. We find

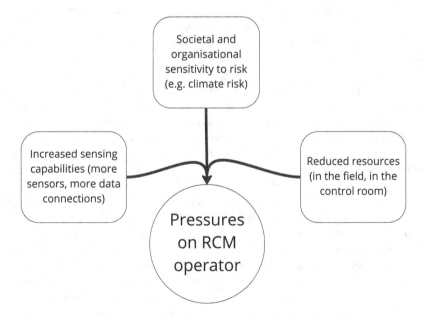

FIGURE 9.3   Growing pressure on RCM operator

the challenges and solutions are still the same. What we hope to do is take the work presented in this work and move from understanding the context and cognition of RCM, to better understand the design and deployment of RCM. This might involve coming up with consistent visual design patterns and metaphors that enable us to convey the information of RCM. Also, as big data and machine learning mature, there is an imperative to communicate not just the outcomes of algorithms, but a sense of the analysis that was performed in order to generate trust in the end user.

Finally, while we have primarily thought about RCM in the desktop environment, there is an ever greater need to take RCM into the field, either to view data on mobile devices or to use mobile devices to augment data.

As we go forward, new tools could be useful. We have touched on the role of workload, but unlike some areas where specific workload tools have been developed already (e.g., Pickup et al. 2010), there are no specific workload tools for RCM users. A tested set of tools would allow not only effective monitoring and quantification of workload in one setting but comparison across multiple settings.

Also, we do not, as yet, have good design and evaluation heuristics. While general heuristics (e.g., https://www.nngroup.com/articles/ten-usability-heuristics/) provide straightforward principles for design, it would be useful to tailor these specifically to the RCM context. It may even be possible to develop specific design patterns and libraries of user interface elements that ensure consistent designs that embed a high level of usability.

The main message here is to embrace technology and what it can provide in the socio-technical context. It is an old problem, and as many before us confirmed, there is a need to change perspectives and approaches to understand both contexts of work and the sequence of elements in these distributed systems. The question is rarely "the why"; most seasoned researchers and engineers agree on the need for this holistic understanding. The challenge is primarily "the how". We have tried to demonstrate that with familiar techniques (observations, interviews, field studies, etc.) and by integrating them, we can learn about what goes in the "magic box". This may not be a complete picture, but it's a very useful start and can give the new technology a decent shot at success. Let's hope this book plays a small role in reimagining our future.

References

Aboelmaged, M. G. (2014). Predicting e-readiness at firm-level: An analysis of technological, organizational and environmental (TOE) effects on e-maintenance readiness in manufacturing firms. *International Journal of Information Management, 34*(5), 639–651.

Adetunji, J. (2011, May). Network rail fined £3m over potters bar crash. *Guardian*, May 13th, 2011.

Adriaens, P., Goovaerts, P., Skerlos, S., Edwards, E., & Egli, T. (2003). Intelligent infrastructure for sustainable potable water: A roundtable for emerging transnational research and technology development needs. *Biotechnology Advances, 22*(1–2), 119–134.

Akhondi, M., Talevski, A., Carlsen, S., & Petersen, S. (2010, April). Applications of wireless sensor networks in the oil, gas and resources industries. In 2010 24th IEEE International Conference on Advanced Information Networking and Applications (pp. 941–948). IEEE.

Aktan, A. E., Helmicki, A. J., & Hunt, V. J. (1998). Issues in health monitoring for intelligent infrastructure. *Smart Materials and Structures, 7*(5), 674.

Aktan, A. E., Catbas, F. N., Grimmelsman,K. A., & Tsikos, C. J. (2000). Issues in infrastructure health monitoring for management. *Journal of Engineering Mechanics*, 126 (7), 711–724.

Armstrong, C. P., & Sambamurthy, V. (1999). Information technology assimilation in firms: The influence of senior leadership and IT infrastructures. *Information Systems Research, 10*(4), 304–327.

Armstrong, J., & Preston, J. (2020, August). Balancing railway network availability and engineering access. In Proceedings of the Institution of Civil Engineers-Transport (Vol. 173, No. 4, pp. 209–217). Thomas Telford Ltd.

Baah, K., Dubey, B., Harvey, R., & McBean, E. (2015). A risk-based approach to sanitary sewer pipe asset management. *Science of the Total Environment, 505*, 1011–1017.

Bainbridge, L. (1983). Ironies of automation. In *Analysis, design and evaluation of man–machine systems* (pp. 129–135). Pergamon.

Bainbridge, L. (1997). The change in concepts needed to account for human behaviour in complex dynamic tasks. *IEEE Transaction on Systems Man and Cybernetics -Part A: Systems and Humans*, 27 (3), 351-359.

Bainbridge, L., & Sanderson, P. (1995). Verbal protocol analysis. In JR Wilson, & EN Corlett (Eds.), *Evaluation of Human Work*: A practical ergonomics methodology (2" ed., pp. 169–201).

Balfe, N., Wilson, J. R., Sharples, S., & Clarke, T. (2012). *Effects of level of signalling automation on workload and performance*. Wilson, J. R., Mills, A., Clarke, T., Rajan, J., & Dadashi, N. (eds.) (pp. 404–411). CRC Press.

Balouchi, F., Bevan, A., & Formston, R. (2021). Development of railway track condition monitoring from multi-train in-service vehicles. *Vehicle System Dynamics, 59*(9), 1397–1417.

Belmonte F, Schön W, Heurley L, Capel R (2011). Interdisciplinary safety analysis of complex socio-technological systems based on the functional resonance accident model: An application to railway traffic supervision. *Reliability Engineering & System Safety, 96*(2), 237–249.

Bernal, E., Spiryagin, M., & Cole, C. (2018). Onboard condition monitoring sensors, systems and techniques for freight railway vehicles: A review. *IEEE Sensors Journal, 19*(1), 4–24.

Bint, M. D. (2008). The role of remote condition monitoring in a modern railway. In 4th IET International Conference on Railway Condition Monitoring (RCM 2008).

Bisantz, A. M., & Drury, C. G. (2005). Applications of archival. *Evaluation of Human Work, 3*, 61-82.

Bisantz, A. M., & Vicente, K. J. (1994). Making the abstraction hierarchy concrete. *International Journal of Human-Computer Studies, 40*(1), 83–117. https://doi.org/10.1006/ijhc.1994.1005

Brown, D. (1999a). Fire Hazards in Tunnels: Changes. Tunnels Management International, (6).

Brown, S. (1999b). The role of alarm systems within safety-related systems-the links with IEC 61508 and IEC 61511. IBC Seminar on Alarm Systems. London: IBC UK Conferences Ltd.

Cacciabue, P. C. (1998). Modelling and simulation of human behaviour for safety analysis and control of complex systems. *Safety Science, 28*(2), 97–110.

Campbell, D. O. (1988). *Characterization of solids in the three mile Island unit 2 reactor defueling water: Addendum (No. ORNL/TM--10362/A1)*. Oak Ridge National Lab.

Carayon, P. (2006). Human factors of complex sociotechnical systems. *Applied Ergonomics, 37*(4), 525–535.

Carretero, J., Pérez, J. M., García-Carballeira, F., Calderón, A., Fernández, J., García, J. D., ..., & Prete, P. (2003). Applying RCM in large scale systems: A case study with railway networks. *Reliability Engineering & System Safety, 82*(3), 257–273.

Chowdhury, S., & Akram, A. (2013). Challenges and opportunities related to remote diagnostics: An IT-based resource perspective. *International Journal of Information Communication Technologies and Human Development (IJICTHD), 5*(3), 80–96.

Ciocoiu, L., Siemieniuch, C., & Hubbard, E. M. (2015). The changes from preventative to predictive maintenance: the organisational challenge.

Ciocoiu, L., Siemieniuch, C. E., & Hubbard, E. M. (2017). From preventative to predictive maintenance: The organisational challenge. *Proceedings of the Institution of Mechanical Engineers, Part F: Journal of Rail and Rapid Transit, 231*(10), 1174–1185.

Coble, J., Ramuhalli, P., Bond, L. J., Hines, J., & Ipadhyaya, B. (2015). A review of prognostics and health management applications in nuclear power plants. *International Journal of Prognostics and Health Management, 6*, 016.

Costello F, & Watts P (2014). Surprisingly rational: Probability theory plus noise explains biases in judgment. *Psychological Review 121*(3):463.

Costello, J. J., West, G. M., & McArthur, S. D. (2017). Machine learning model for event-based prognostics in gas circulator condition monitoring. *IEEE Transactions on Reliability, 66*(4), 1048–1057.

Crainic, T. G., Gendreau, M., & Potvin, J.-Y. (2009). Intelligent freight-transportation systems: Assessment and the contribution of operations research. *Transportation Research Part C: Emerging Technologies, 17*(6), 541–557. Elsevier Ltd.

Cullen, L. (2000). *The Ladbroke Grove rail inquiry, Part 1 report*. HSE Books, HMSO.

Dadashi, N., Wilson, J. R., Sharples, S., Golightly, D., & Clarke, T. (2010). Fault analysis in railway maintenance control centres. In International control room design conference, ICOCO. Paris-France.

Dadashi, N., Wilson, J. R., Golightly, D., & Sharples, S. (2014). A framework to support human factors of automation in railway intelligent infrastructure. *Ergonomics, 57*(3), 387–402.

Dadashi, N., Golightly, D., & Sharples, S. (2017). Seeing the woods for the trees: The problem of information inefficiency and information overload on operator performance. *Cognition, Technology & Work, 19*(4), 561–570.

Dadashi, N., Golightly, D., & Sharples, S. (2021). Modelling decision-making within rail maintenance control rooms. *Cognition, Technology & Work, 23*, 255-271.

Dekker, S. (2004). *Ten questions about human error: A new view of human factors and system safety.* CRC Press.

Diyan, M., Nathali Silva, B., Han, J., Cao, Z., & Han, K. (2020). Intelligent Internet of Things gateway supporting heterogeneous energy data management and processing. *Transactions on Emerging Telecommunications Technologies*, e3919.

Dorgo, G., Varga, K., Haragovics, M., Szabo, T., & Abonyi, J. (2018). Towards operator 4.0, increasing production efficiency and reducing operator workload by process mining of alarm data. *Chemical Engineering Transactions*, *70*, 829–834.

Durazo-Cardenas, I., Starr, A., Turner, C. J., Tiwari, A., Kirkwood, L., Bevilacqua, M., ..., & Emmanouilidis, C. (2018). An autonomous system for maintenance scheduling data-rich complex infrastructure: Fusing the railways' condition, planning and cost. *Transportation Research Part C: Emerging Technologies*, *89*, 234–253.

The Engineering Equipment and Materials Users Association (EEMUA) (1999). *Alarm systems: A guide to design management and procurement – EEMUA publication No. 191*, ISBN 0 85931 076 0.

Endsley, M. R. (1995). Toward a theory of situation awareness in dynamic systems. *Human factors*, *37*(1), 32–64.

Ericsson, K. A. (2006). Protocol analysis and expert thought: Concurrent verbalizations of thinking during experts' performance on representative tasks. In *The Cambridge handbook of expertise and expert performance* (223–241).

European Rail Research Advisory Council (2017). Rail 2050 Vision: Rail: The Backbone of Europe's mobility. http://www.errac.org/wp-content/uploads/2018/01/122017_ERRAC -RAIL-2050.pdfRSSBstrategy. Accessed 20 Sept 2019.

Farrington-Darby, T., Pickup, L., & Wilson, J. R. (2005). Safety culture in railway maintenance. *Safety Science*, *43*(1), 39–60.

Feltovich, P. J., Hoffman, R. R., Woods, D., & Roesler, A. (2004). Keeping it too simple: How the reductive tendency affects cognitive engineering. *IEEE Intelligent Systems*, *19*(3), 90–94.

Fidel, R., & Pejtersen, A. (2004). From information behaviour research to the design of information systems: The Cognitive Work Analysis framework. *Information Research*, *10*(1), 210.

Flach, J. M. (2012). Complexity: Learning to muddle through. *Cognition, Technology & Work*, *14*(3), 187–197.

Fuld, R. B. (1993). The fiction of function allocation. *Ergonomics in Design*, *1*(1), 20–24.

Garcia Marquez, F. P., Roberts, C., & Tobias, A. M. (2007). Railway point mechanisms: Condition monitoring and fault detection. *Rail and Rapid Transit*, 35–44.

Ghofrani, A., Nazemi, S. D., & Jafari, M. A. (2020). Prediction of building indoor temperature response in variable air volume systems. *Journal of Building Performance Simulation*, *13*(1), 34–47.

Gilson, R. D., Mouloua, M., Graft, A. S., & McDonald, D. P. (2001). Behavioral influences of proximal alarms. *Human Factors*, *43*(4), 595–610.

Golightly, D., & Dadashi, N. (2017). The characteristics of railway service disruption: Implications for disruption management. *Ergonomics*, *60*(3), 307–320.

Golightly, D., & Palacin, R. (2021). Human Factors contribution to rail decarbonisation. In 7th International Rail Human Factors Conference. Newcastle University.

Golightly, D., & Young, M. S. (2022). Local knowledge in rail signalling and balancing trade-offs. *Applied Ergonomics*, *102*, 103714.

Golightly, D., Wilson, J. R., Lowe, E., & Sharples, S. (2010). The role of situation awareness for understanding signalling and control in rail operations. *Theoretical Issues in Ergonomics Science*, *11*(1–2), 84–98.

Golightly, D., Ryan, B., Dadashi, N., Pickup, L., & Wilson, J. R. (2013a). Use of scenarios and function analyses to understand the impact of situation awareness on safe and effective work on rail tracks. *Safety Science*, *56*, 52–62.

Golightly, D., Dadashi, N., Sharples, S., & Dasigi, M. (2013b). Disruption management processes during emergencies on the railways. *International Journal of Human Factors and Ergonomics, 2*(2–3), 175–195.

Golightly, D., Kefalidou, G., & Sharples, S. (2018). A cross-sector analysis of human and organisational factors in the deployment of data-driven predictive maintenance. *Information Systems and e-Business Management, 16*(3), 627–648.

Groppe, M., Pagliari, R., & Harris, D. (2009, March). Applying cognitive work analysis to study airport collaborative decision making design. In Proceedings of the ENRI International Workshop on ATM/CNS (pp. 77–88).

Grubic, T. (2018). Remote monitoring technology and servitization: Exploring the relationship. *Computers in Industry, 100*, 148–158.

Guldenmund, F. W. (2000). The nature of safety culture: a review of theory and research. *Safety Science,* 34(1-3), 215–257.

Health and Safety Executive Board, H. P. B. I. (2003). *Train derailment at potters bar 10 may 2002.* Office of Rail Regulation.

Hoffman, R. R., & Woods, D. D. (Eds.) (2000). Cognitive task analysis [special issue]. *Human Factors, 42*, 1–95.

Hollnagel, E. (2012). Coping with complexity: past, present and future. *Cognition, Technology & Work, 14*(3), 199–205.

Hollnagel, E. (2017). Why is work-as-imagined different from work-as-done?. In *Resilient health care* (Vol. 2, pp. 279–294). CRC Press.

Hollnagel, E., & Woods, D. D. (2005). *Joint cognitive systems: Foundations of cognitive systems engineering.* CRC Press.

Hollnagel, E., Wears, R. L., & Braithwaite, J. (2015). From Safety-I to Safety-II: a white paper. The resilient health care net: published simultaneously by the University of Southern Denmark, University of Florida, USA, and Macquarie University, Australia.

Houghton, R. J., & Patel, H. (2015, August). Interface design for prognostic asset maintenance. In Proceedings 19th Triennial Congress of the IEA (Vol. 9, p. 14).

Hutchins, E. (1995). *Cognition in the Wild.* The MIT Press.

International Energy Agency (2019). *The future of rail. Opportunities for energy and the environment.* IEA Publications. https://webstore.iea.org/the-future-of-rail

ISO 9241-210 (2010). Ergonomics of human-system interaction – Part 210: Human-centred design for interactive systems. 2015. [Accessed March 18, 2015]. Available from: http://www.iso.org/iso/home/store/catalogue_ics/catalogue_detail_ics.htm?csnumber =52075.

ISO 11064-4:2013 (2013). *Ergonomics design of control centers-Part 4: Layout and dimensions of workstations.* ISO.

ISO 13374-4 (2015). Condition monitoring and diagnostics of machine systems — Data processing, communication and presentation — Part 4: Presentation. https://www.iso.org/standard/54933.html.

ISO/IEC TR 22417 (2017). *Information technology-Internet of things (IOT).* ISO.

Jang, B., & Lee, J. (2017). Study on the maintenance interval decisions for life expectancy in railway turnout clearance detector. *Journal of the Korean Society for Railway, 20*(4), 491–499.

Jansson, A., Olsson, E., & Erlandsson, M. (2006). Bridging the gap between analysis and design: Improving existing driver interfaces with tools from the framework of cognitive work analysis. *Cognition, Technology & Work, 8*(1), 41–49.

Jing, G., Siahkouhi, M., Qian, K., & Wang, S. (2021). Development of a field condition monitoring system in high speed railway turnout. *Measurement, 169*, 108358.

Josey, J. (2013). Intelligent infrastructure for next‑ generation rail system. *Cognizant 2020 Insights*, 1–8.

Kaber, D. B., & Endsley, M. R. (2004). The effects of level of automation and adaptive automation on human performance, situation awareness and workload in a dynamic control task. *Theoretical Issues in Ergonomics Science, 5*(2), 113–153.

Kajko-Mattsson, M., Azizyan, G., & Magarian, M. K. (2010, August). Classes of distributed agile development problems. In 2010 Agile Conference (pp. 51–58). IEEE.

Kaul, C., Smyth, J., & Patrick, C. (2022). Predicting the impact of future decarbonisation strategy on railway electrical control rooms. *Contemporary Ergonomics & Human Factors*, 345–355.

Kefalidou, G., Golightly, D., & Sharples, S. (2015). Understanding factors for design and deployment of predictive maintenance. In Proceedings of 5th International Rail Human Factors Conference, London, September 2015.

Kefalidou, G., Golightly, D., & Sharples, S. (2018). Identifying rail asset maintenance processes: A human-centric and sensemaking approach. *Cognition, Technology & Work, 20*(1), 73–92.

Khan, A. M. (2007). Intelligent infrastructure-based queue-end warning system for avoiding rear impacts. *IET International Transport Systems, 2*, 138–143.

Kim, D., & Yoon, W. C. (2013). An accident causation model for the railway industry: Application of the model to 80 rail accident investigation reports from the UK. *Safety Science, 60*, 57–68.

Klein, G. A., Calderwood, R., & Macgregor, D. (1989). Critical decision method for eliciting knowledge. *IEEE Transactions on Systems, Man, and Cybernetics, 19*(3), 462–472.

Ko, J. M., & Ni, Y. Q. (2005). Technology developments in structural health monitoring of large-scale bridges. *Engineering Structures, 27*(12), 1715–1725.

Koenig, F., Found, P. A., & Kumar, M. (2019). Condition monitoring for airport baggage handling in the era of industry 4.0. *Journal of Quality in Maintenance Engineering. 25*(3), 435–451.

Koochaki, J., & Bouwhuis, I. M. (2008, December). The role of knowledge sharing and Transactive Memory System on Condition Based Maintenance policy. In 2008 IEEE International Conference on Industrial Engineering and Engineering Management (pp. 32–36). IEEE.

Kurup, S., Golightly, D., Clarke, D., & Sharples, S. (2021). Passenger information provision: Perspectives from rail industry stakeholders in Great Britain. *Journal of Rail Transport Planning & Management, 19*, 100264.

Lau, Henry, Ip, R., & Chan, F. (2002). An intelligent information infrastructure to support knowledge discovery. *Expert Systems with Applications 22*, 1–10.

Li, R., & He, D. (2012). Rotational machine health monitoring and fault detection using EMD-based acoustic emission feature quantification. *IEEE Transactions on Instrumentation and Measurement, 61*(4), 990–1001.

Lintern, G. (2009). The foundation and pragmatics of cognitive work analysis: A systematic approach to design of large-scale information systems. Dayton, OH: Cognitive Systems Design. Retrieved from http://www.cognitivesystemsdesign.net/Downloads/ Foundations & Pragmatics of CWA.

Liu, S., Chen, H., Shang, B., & Papanikolaou, A. (2022). Supporting Predictive Maintenance of a Ship by Analysis of Onboard Measurements. *Journal of Marine Science and Engineering, 10*(2), 215.

Mack, Z., & Sharples, S. (2009). The importance of usability in product choice: A mobile phone case study. *Ergonomics, 52*(12), 1514–1528.

Mayer, A. K., Fisk, A. D., & Rogers, W. A. (2009). *Understanding technology acceptance: Effects of user expectancies on human-automation interaction.* Georgia Institute of Technology.

Mayer, M. P., Schlick, C. M., Ewert, D., Behnen, D., Kuz, S., Odenthal, B., & Kausch, B. (2011). Automation of robotic assembly processes on the basis of an architecture of human cognition. *Production Engineering, 5*(4), 423–431.

McNulty, Sir R (2011). *Realising the potential of GB Rail: Final independent report of the Rail Value for Money study.* Department for Transport and Office of Rail Regulation.

McRoberts, P. (2018). Improve energy management with intelligent packaged power. *Engineering and Mining Journal, 219*(9), 56–57.

Mikkonen, H., & Lahdelma, S. (2014). Remote monitoring allows new operating practices in condition monitoring. In 11th International Conference on Condition Monitoring and Machinery Failure Prevention Technologies–CM/MFPT.

Miles, M. B., & Huberman, A. M. (1994). *Qualitative data analysis: An expanded sourcebook.* Sage.

Millen, L., Edwards, T., Golightly, D., Sharples, S., Wilson, J. R., & Kirwan, B. (2011). Systems change in transport control: Applications of cognitive work analysis. *The International Journal of Aviation Psychology, 21*(1), 62–84.

Mogles, N., Walker, I., Ramallo-González, A. P., Lee, J., Natarajan, S., Padget, J., ..., & Coley, D. (2017). How smart do smart meters need to be?. *Building and Environment, 125*, 439–450.

Mynatt, E., Clark, J., Hager, G., Lopresti, D., Morrisett, G., Nahrstedt, K., ..., & Zorn, B. (2017). *A national research agenda for intelligent infrastructure. arXiv preprint arXiv:1705.01920.*

NAO (National Audit Office) (2008). *Reducing passenger rail delays by better management of incidents: Report, together with formal minutes, oral and written evidence* (Vol. 655). HMSO.

Neale, H., & Nichols, S. (2001). Theme-based content analysis: A flexible method for virtual environment evaluation. *International Journal of Human-computer Studies, 55*(2), 167–189.

Negenborn, R. R., Lukszo, Z., Hollendoorn., H. (Eds) (2010). *Intelligent infrastructure.* Springer.

Network Rail. (2009). *Network rail intelligent infrastructure strategy.* Network Rail.

Nielsen, K. (2020). Preferences for the resolution of uncertainty and the timing of information. *Journal of Economic Theory, 189*, 105090.

NUREG-0711: Rev.1 Human Factors Engineering Program Review Model

Oborski, P. (2004). Man-machine interactions in advanced manufacturing systems. *The International Journal of Advanced Manufacturing Technology, 23*(3), 227–232.

O'Hare, D. A. V. I. D., Wiggins, M., Williams, A., & Wong, W. (1998). Cognitive task analyses for decision centred design and training. *Ergonomics, 41*(11), 1698–1718.

Ollier, B. D. (2006). Intelligent Infrastructure the business challenge. In International Conference on Railway Condition Monitoring, The Institution of Engineering and Technology

Ottens, M., Franssen, M., Kroes, P., & Van De Poel, I. (2006). Modelling infrastructures as socio-technical systems. *International Journal of Critical Infrastructures, 2*(2–3), 133–145.

Ouelhadj, D., & Petrovic, S. (2009). A survey of dynamic scheduling in manufacturing systems. *Journal of Scheduling, 12*(4), 417–431.

Park, H., Barrett, A., Baumann, E., Grage, M., & Narasimhan, S. (2006). Modular architecture for hybrid diagnostic reasoners. In Second IEEE International Conference on Space Mission Challenges for Information Technology, SMC-IT 2006.

Petkov, N., Wu, H., & Powell, R. (2020). Cost-benefit analysis of condition monitoring on DEMO remote maintenance system. *Fusion Engineering and Design, 160*, 112022.

Patel, H., Pettitt, M., & Wilson, J. R. (2012). Factors of collaborative working: A framework for a collaboration model. *Applied Ergonomics*, 43(1), 1–26.

Pew, R. W., & Mavor, A. S. (2007). Human-system integration in the system development process: A new look. In *Methods for evaluation*. National Academies Press. pp.267–74.

Pickup, L., Wilson, J. R., Norris, B. J., Mitchell, L., & Morrisroe, G. (2005). The Integrated Workload Scale (IWS): A new self-report tool to assess railway signaller workload. *Applied Ergonomics*, 36(6), 681–693.

Pickup, L., Wilson, J., & Lowe, E. (2010). The Operational Demand Evaluation Checklist (ODEC) of workload for railway signalling. *Applied Ergonomics*, 41(3), 393–402.

Pickup, L., Balfe, N., Lowe, E., & Wilson, J. R. (2013). He's not from around here: The significance of local knowledge. *Rail Human Factors: Supporting reliability, safety and cost reduction*, 357 357–369.

RAE (2012). Royal Academy of Engineering (1 https://www.raeng.org.uk/publications/reports/smart-infrastructure-the-future).

Rankin, A., Lundberg, J., Woltjer, R., Rollenhagen, C., & Hollnagel, E. (2014). Resilience in everyday operations: A framework for analyzing adaptations in high-risk work. *Journal of Cognitive Engineering and Decision Making*, 8(1), 78–97.

Rail Accident Investigation Branch. (2008). *Rail accident report, derailment at Grayrigg, 23 February 2007* (p. 256). Retrieved from http://www.raib.gov.uk/cms_resources.cfm?file=/081023_R202008_Grayrigg_v4r.pdf.

Ramchurn, S. D., Vytelingum, P., Rogers, A., & Jennings, N. R. (2012). Putting the'smarts' into the smart grid: A grand challenge for artificial intelligence. *Communications of the ACM*, 55(4), 86–97.

Ramchurn, S. D., Wu, F., Jiang, W., Fischer, J. E., Reece, S., Roberts, S., ... & Jennings, N. R. (2016). Human–agent collaboration for disaster response. *Autonomous Agents and Multi-Agent Systems*, 30, 82–111.

Rasmussen, J. (1985). The role of hierarchical knowledge representation in decision making and system management. *IEEE Transactions on Systems, Man, and Cybernetics*, SMC-15(2), 234–243. https://doi.org/10.1109/TSMC.1985.6313353

Rasmussen, J. (1986). A framework for cognitive task analysis in systems design. In *Intelligent decision support in process environments* (pp. 175–196). Springer.

Rasmussen, J. (1997). Risk management in a dynamic society: A modelling problem. *Safety Science*, 27(2), 183–213.

Rasmussen, J., & Lind, M. (1982, June). A model of human decision making in complex systems and its use for design of system control strategies. In 1982 American Control Conference (pp. 270–276). IEEE.

Rasmussen, J, Pejtersen, A. M., & Goodstein, L. P. (1994). *Cognitive system engineering*. John Wiley & Sons, Inc.

Reason, J. (1990). *Human error*. Cambridge University Press.

Reising, D. V. C., & Sanderson, P. M. (1998, October). Designing displays under ecological interface design: Towards operationalizing semantic mapping. In Proceedings of the Human Factors and Ergonomics Society Annual Meeting (Vol. 42, No. 3, pp. 372–376). SAGE Publications.

Riley, D. (2006). Manual Handling in the Rail Sector in South Wales. HSL/2006/53.

Robson, C., & McCartan, K. (2016). *Real world research*. Wiley Global Education.

Rolo, G., & Diaz-Cabrera, D. (2005). Decision-making processes evaluation using two methodologies: Field and simulation techniques. *Theoretical Issues in Ergonomics Science*, 6(1), 35–48.

Rosson, M. B., & Carroll, J. M. (2009). Scenario based design. *Human-computer Interaction*, 161–180. CRC Press.

Ryan, B., Golightly, D., Pickup, L., Reinartz, S., Atkinson, S., & Dadashi, N. (2021). Human functions in safety-developing a framework of goals, human functions and safety relevant activities for railway socio-technical systems. *Safety Science, 140*, 105279.

Sanderson, P., Naikar, N., Lintern, G., & Goss, S. (1999, September). Use of cognitive work analysis across the system life cycle: From requirements to decommissioning. In Proceedings of the Human Factors and Ergonomics Society Annual Meeting (Vol. 43, No. 3, pp. 318–322). SAGE Publications.

Sebok, A., & Wickens, C. D. (2017). Implementing lumberjacks and black swans into model-based tools to support human–automation interaction. *Human Factors, 59*(2), 189–203.

Schock, A., Ryan, B., Wilson, J., Clarke, T., & Sharples, S. (2010). Visual scenario analysis: Understanding human factors of planning in rail engineering. *Production Planning and Control, 21*(4), 386–398.

Schrom, H., Schwartze, J., & Diekmann, S. (2017, September). Building automation by an intelligent embedded infrastructure: Combining medical, smart energy, smart environment and heating. In 2017 International Smart Cities Conference (ISC2) (pp. 1–4). IEEE.

Sharples, S., Millen, L., Golightly, D., & Balfe, N. (2011). The impact of automation in rail signalling operations. *Proceedings of the Institution of Mechanical Engineers, Part F: Journal of Rail and Rapid Transit, 225*(2), 179–191.

Sheng, S. (2017). *Wind turbine gearbox reliability database, operation and maintenance research update* (No. NREL/PR-5000-68347). National Renewable Energy Lab. (NREL).

Shepherd, A., & Stammers, R. B. (2005). Task analysis. In Wilson, J. & Corlett, E. N. (Eds.)*Evaluation of Human Work*, (3rd ed., pp. 129–158). Boca Raton, FL: CRC Press.

Sheridan, T. B. (1997). Task analysis, task allocation and supervisory control. In *Handbook of human-computer interaction* (pp. 87–105). North-Holland.

Sheridan, T. B., & Hennessy, R. T. (1984). *Research and modeling of supervisory control behavior. Report of a workshop*. National Research Council Washington DC Committee on Human Factors.

Sheridan, T. B., Sheridan, T. B., Maschinenbauingenieur, K., Sheridan, T. B., & Sheridan, T. B. (2002). *Humans and automation: System design and research issues* (Vol. 280). Human Factors and Ergonomics Society.

Shorrock, S., & Williams, C. (2016). *Human factors and ergonomics in practice: Improving system performance and human well-being in the real world*. CRC Press.

Smith, D. J. (2013) Power-by-the-hour: The role of technology in reshaping business strategy at Rolls-Royce. *Technology Analysis and Strategic Management, 25*(8), 987–1007.

Standard, B., & ISO, B. (2001). Ergonomic design of control centres.". BS EN ISO, 11064-1.

Stanton, N. A. (2006). Alarm initiated activities. In Karwowski W (ed) *International encyclopaedia of ergonomics and human factors* (2nd ed., pp. 1008–1011). Taylor & Francis.

Stanton, N.A., & Baber, C. (2006). The ergonomics of command and control. *Ergonomics, 49*(12–13), 1131–1138.

Stanton, N. A., & Stammers, R. B. (1998). *Alarm initiated activities: Matching formats to tasks*.

Stanton, N. A., Salmon, P. M., & Rafferty, L. A. (2013). *Human factors methods: A practical guide for engineering and design*. Ashgate Publishing, Ltd.

Strasunskas, D. (2006). Resource monitoring and rule-based notification. Applications in subsea production systems. *Information Systems*, 74–91.

Sundh, J., & Juslin, P. (2018). Compound risk judgment in tasks with both idiosyncratic and systematic risk: The "Robust Beauty" of additive probability integration. *Cognition, 171*, 25–41.

Sundstrom, G. A., & Salvador, A. C. (1995). Integrating field work in system design: A methodology and two case studies. *IEEE Transactions on Systems, Man, and Cybernetics, 25*(3), 385–399.

Szymula, C., & Bešinović, N. (2020). Passenger-centered vulnerability assessment of railway networks. *Transportation Research Part B: Methodological, 136*, 30–61.

Tarrant, O., Hambidge, C., Hollingsworth, C., Normandale, D., & Burdett, S. (2018). Identifying the signs of weakness, deterioration, and damage to flood defence infrastructure from remotely sensed data and mapped information. *Journal of Flood Risk Management, 11*(3), 317–330.

Timms, C. (2009). Hazards equal trips or alarms or both. *Process Safety and Environmental Protection, 87*(1), 3–13.

Tokody, D., Albini, A., Ady, L., Rajnai, Z., & Pongrácz, F. (2018). Safety and security through the design of autonomous intelligent vehicle systems and intelligent infrastructure in the smart city. *Interdisciplinary Description of Complex Systems: INDECS, 16*(3-A), 384–396.

Trist, E. (1981). The evolution of socio-technical systems. *Occasional Paper, 2*(1981), 1981.

UN (United Nations) (2018) *2018 revision of world urbanisation prospects.* UN Population Division.

Vaghefi, K., Oats, R. C., Harris, D. K., Ahlborn, T. T. M., Brooks, C. N., Endsley, K. A., ..., & Dobson, R. (2012). Evaluation of commercially available remote sensors for highway bridge condition assessment. *Journal of Bridge Engineering, 17*(6), 886–895.

Vicente, K. J. (1999). *Cognitive work analysis: Toward safe, productive, and healthy computer-based work.* CRC Press.

Vileiniskis, M., Remenyte-Prescott, R., & Rama, D. (2016). A fault detection method for railway point systems. *Proceedings of the Institution of Mechanical Engineers, Part F: Journal of Rail and Rapid Transit, 230*(3), 852–865.

Vinberg, E. M., Martin, M., Firdaus, A. H., Tang, Y., & Qazizadeh, A. (2018). *Railway applications of condition monitoring.* KTH Royal Institute of Technology.

Warm, J. S., Parasuraman, R., & Matthews, G. (2008). Vigilance requires hard mental work and is stressful. *Human Factors, 50*(3), 433–441.

Whelan, M. J., Gangone, M. V., & Janoyan, K. D. (2009). Highway bridge assessment using an adaptive real-time wireless sensor network. *IEEE Sensors Journal, 9*(11), 1405–1413.

Wickens, C. D., Gordon, S. E., Liu, Y., & Lee, J. (2004). *An introduction to human factors engineering* (Vol. 2). Pearson Prentice Hall.

Wilkinson, J., & Lucas, D. (2002). Better alarm handling: A practical application of human factors. *Measurement and Control, 35*(2), 52–54.

Wilson, J. R. (2014). Fundamentals of systems ergonomics/human factors. *Applied Ergonomics, 45*(1), 5–13.

Wilson, J. R., & Sharples, S. (2015). *Evaluation of human work.* CRC Press.

Wu, L., Zhu, Z., Cao, H., & Li, B. (2016). Influence of information overload on operator's user experience of human–machine interface in LED manufacturing systems. *Cognition, Technology & Work, 18*(1), 161–173.

Index

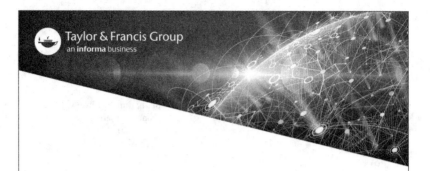

Printed in the United States
by Baker & Taylor Publisher Services